IS PEACE INEVITABLE?

Aggression, Evolution, and Human Destiny

SANTIAGO GENOVES

*with an Introduction
by Theodosius Dobzhansky*

WALKER AND COMPANY • New York

U
22.3
.Ʉ4513
1970

First published in Spanish in a slightly different version as Number 81 in the Nueva Colección Labor, published by Editorial Labor, Barcelona, under the title *El hombre entre la guerra y la paz*. Copyright © Editorial Labor, SA. Deposito legal B. 22932-68.

First published in the United States of America in 1970 by the Walker Publishing Company, Inc.

Published simultaneously in Canada by The Ryerson Press, Toronto.

ISBN: 0-8027-0322-4

Library of Congress Catalog Card Number: 79-126113

Printed in the United States of America.

Book designed by Lena Fong Hor

ADAM THE INVENTOR

Early in the morning,
Just as the sun was rising,
Adam started inventing things
And the results were surprising.

> Later in the morning,
> The sun was getting higher.
> Adam made a discovery—
> He learned to handle fire.

He invented spears; invented guns,
Invented arrow and bow.
And what is it next he will invent?
I'm not sure I want to know.

> Invented language, invented words,
> Invented the alphabet,
> But when it comes to communicating
> Sometimes he was deaf.

You conquered desert, conquered ice,
Conquered ocean and shore,
Conquered every animal except yourself—
It's you that invented war.

> Adam, brilliant Adam,
> So brilliant, you're made blind
> Inventing some new kind of world
> With no place for mankind.

Stamp your foot, we've just one earth,
One big red apple to share,
All around one ocean of water
And just one ocean of air.

> Can we break the grip of the Dance of Death?
> Can this world be released?
> Will Adam's children, the young inventors,
> Will they now invent peace?

And some will scoff, and some will scorn
But what makes them so God damn certain?
Adam's children might surprise them all
And build anew the garden.

Words by Pete Seeger, Santiago Genovés,
and Wolf Rilla
Music by Pete Seeger

CONTENTS

For Andrée and Diego

INTRODUCTION

Professor Genovés is one of the relatively rare research scientists who are able to write accounts of their
science for popular audiences. His book is a populari-
zation at its best: it probes deeply into its subject matter, it does not talk down to the reader, and it is
surprisingly free of technical jargon. Most important, it
deals with problems of great concern in the modern
world—racism, aggression, and war.

All men may have been created equal, but surely they
have not been created all alike. In point of fact, no two
persons, excepting only "identical" twins, are biologically, genetically, identical. Every individual is provided
with a unique, unprecedented, and unrepeatable
hereditary endowment. We have to live in a world with
a multitude of other people, all different from ourselves
and from other people. Must the differences necessarily lead to conflict among people, just because they
are different? Has biological and anthropological research invalidated the doctrine of human equality?
Professor Genovés shows that this is not so. Equality is
not a deduction from biological studies. It is an ethical
precept, a religious commandment, a social policy. No
society can make its members biologically alike, even if
this were desirable, which is surely not so. A society
can, however, bestow an equality of opportunity, equal-

ity before the law, and equal respect for the human dignity of every human individual, regardless of the genetic diversity. By the same token, societies exist in which people are grossly unequal economically, or in their social position or caste status, and this again regardless of how similar or different they may be in their genetic endowments. Equality does not mean that everybody must be made exactly alike; such enforced sameness would do violence to the diversity of human traits and preferences. Democracy is an acknowledgment of the freedom of human individuals to choose different courses of self-actualization, limited only by the necessity to prevent interference with the freedom of other individuals. This can be achieved best by cooperation rather than by competition, by peace rather than by war. Professor Genovés firmly rejects the claims of some pseudo-scientists, who allege that man is aggressive by nature, and endowed with something called territorial imperative or a drive for domination and subjugation of other men. Aggression is learned, not inborn or biologically necessary. War is a social disease, not an adaptation. It can and must be avoided, despite the incitements coming from the various pentagons, East and West.

Theodosius Dobzhansky

PREFACE TO THE U.S. EDITION

This book is about war and the various theories designed to explain or excuse it. Most of these theories involve some kind of appeal to evidence drawn from psychology, on the one hand, and genetics, on the other. In recent years appeals to the growing science of animal behavior, or ethology, have become increasingly fashionable. Sometimes it appears as if the only science that is of no use in explaining war is anthropology, the study of human biology and of human culture.

I am an anthropologist—a physical anthropologist, specializing in the development of early man. To me such statements as "Man is aggressive," or "Man is the most dangerous animal," sound strange and ambiguous. People generally think of physical anthropologists as spending their time digging up and measuring bones. This is partly true. But the lesson that these bones teach is that man *evolves.* So I have what might be called an acquired incapacity to believe that man "is" this or that one thing for all eternity.

Man also has a culture, of which war is part. I do not know if any other animal species can be said to have a culture, but if it can the culture is surely a rather uncomplicated one compared to ours. That is another reason why I and so many of my colleagues in the social sciences find direct comparisons between men and animals somewhat beside the point. But, above all, I do not believe that animals behave very much like men. The crucial differentiating factor is the human culture, which is itself evolving all the time.

This book originated as background research for a film called *PAX?* that I made at the request of the Organizing Committee of the Nineteenth Olympic Games, celebrated in Mexico in 1968. I would like to take this opportunity to once more thank the Committee, especially its chairman, Pedro Ramírez Vazquez, for setting me such a congenial task. I have long been convinced that peace is not merely the absence of war, and still less a kind of eternal sleep, but rather a state of actively striving to excel. Viewed in an evolutionary perspective, the institution of the original Olympic Games was a turning point in the history of culture; for the first time, man dedicated himself to a playful use of his strength.*

Perhaps something of this sort was on my mind when I joined Thor Heyerdahl and his international crew on the RA I in 1969, and again on the RA II the following year. Crossing the Atlantic in a papyrus vessel of prehistoric design certainly wasn't easy or safe. But to me

*I have expressed these ideas in another film, *Muscle and Culture,* a seven-minute animated cartoon awarded a diploma by the Mexican Centro Cultural Cinematográfico in 1969.

the most exciting thing about it was the chance it of-
fered to see if a small group of men drawn from totally
diverse cultures and backgrounds could cooperate under such circumstances.

Well, cooperate we did. Ever since then, people have
been asking me why I, a middle-aged scientific researcher and family man, found it worthwhile to take
part in such a risky enterprise. To which I usually try to
reply that peace is the most risky enterprise of all, and
also the most worthwhile.

Among the many persons who helped to make this
book and its related activities possible, special mention
should be made of Joaquín Cortina, Department of
Cultural Diffusion of the INAH, Mexico; Roberto
MacLean, Derecho Internacional Privado, Peru; and
José Mora, Spain. In 1969 the Barcelona chapter of *Pax
Christi* honored the Spanish edition of this work with
the Pope John XXIII Memorial Prize. John Paddock,
archaeologist at the Centro de Estudios Científicos
Oaxaqueños, made valuable comments on the Spanish
edition, many of which have been incorporated in the
present one. It was Sol Tax of the University of Chicago
who urged me to prepare an English-language edition
in the first place. J.M.B. Edwards, of Palo Alto, California, adapted my all too literal translation to its present form, undertook other editorial chores while I was
on RA II, and even found me a New York publisher—
a very congenial one, I should add. Finally, I am most
grateful to Theodosius Dobzhansky for writing the in-

troduction; my debt to his thinking will be evident from the following pages. To these, and to the many others who made possible this particular experiment in international cooperation, my heartfelt thanks.

S.G.

1

WAR THE ABSURD

Our own history, at least the part of it that we know best, is a chronicle of armed conflicts and frustrated peace efforts. Between 1920 and 1963 wars, in the fullest sense of the word, occurred at the rate of one a year.[1] On the other hand, the history of peace in our time seems to be nothing more than a series of successive substitutions of one impractical dream for another, each quickly ending in failure. It is enough, for example, to examine the list of Nobel Prize winners to perceive that while the majority of persons awarded prizes in science and (on occasion) in literature still continue to be remembered with admiration, the list of persons awarded the Peace Prize is made up of names which today are largely forgotten, when not actually objects of scepticism or ridicule.

IS PEACE INEVITABLE?

What is it, then, that has failed in the idea of peace? Naturally we can hardly expect to find a set of infallible formula to answer this question and end all wars forthwith. But we can begin by suggesting that peace is too often conceived as a static and more or less beatific state of inaction. Perhaps this is because we tend to think of it as existing in a distant "then and there," far removed from the immediate "here and now." Or perhaps we hope for the miraculous cessation of all historical change; we want to renounce progress in order to enjoy a peace that is really a negation of all effort. To think of peace in such a manner is to abjure it. For change is with us everywhere in this world, and a way of life based on resistance to change leads inevitably to violence and the use of force.

It can also be argued that to conceive peace as the absence of effort is to have nothing on hand to counter the pessimism of those who believe that peace is impossible; indeed, it is to play into the hands of those who believe war is beautiful or glorious. It would seem necessary, then, if the possibilities of a real peace are to be examined, not to withdraw from those fields of argument where pessimism and bellicosity have already formed ranks. We must search for peace in the real world.

IS WAR INEVITABLE?

Since all wars have their origins in peace, it follows that peace, however transitory, has existed as often as war. There is, therefore, no reason for declaring as Ardrey has that war is a natural phenomenon, while peace is only an idealistic invention.[2] Our natural tendencies demonstrate the contrary; peace, like health, though never perfect and complete, seems to us a natural condition, and a positive state of things, whereas war, like sickness, is seen by us as an abnormal state and a negative state of things. So Montesquieu said that peace is "the first law of Nature."

Because of this, although we may hardly aspire to a solution of a problem that has eluded humanity for so many centuries, we cannot afford to abandon the world of facts in order to postulate an ideal that no one knows how to translate into reality. This book was written in the belief that it is possible to assemble, if only on a small scale, certain facts that are pertinent to a discussion of peace in this world of change, tensions, and conflicts. If war is no longer what it was, then neither is peace and neither are the chances for peace. Many of today's ethnologists and anthropologists are inclined to look on war as a phenomenon linked to definite periods of history and certain forms of human society. There is nothing to prevent war from being a phenomenon which appears at a given moment in time and disappears at another, in the same way as many other human activities. War, then, like so many other things which once seemed immutable laws, might be just a stage in the history of human progress.

It is always hazardous to determine what is natural and what is artificial, or to be more scientific, what is due to biology and what to culture—especially since human nature, as it has evolved, is a cultural product. It is well known that most of mankind is reluctant to accept its inclusion in the biological realm as just another animal species. But all unfamiliar truths meet this kind of resistance. The fact that our planet is not the center of the universe gained general acceptance only after much persecution and bloodshed; primitive mythologies always present the world as a flat expanse, with its center occupied by whatever tribe is the subject of the myth. In the same way, much ink, if not blood, has flowed since certain men first began to suspect that the species *sapiens* was not, after all, a member of an order different from all other living things, but rather just another of the many forms of life that exist on our planet.

And yet where war is concerned, these reactions seem to be forgotten. No one who has wished to glorify or even simply to justify war has ever shrunk from comparisons, examples and even mistaken deductions taken from the animal kingdom. Frequently the same persons who became indignant at the suggestion that their species, man, should no longer be considered the lord of creation, for whom the world was specially created and expressly organized down to the smallest detail, are the very ones who consider war as man's most brilliant ornament. And, in their untiring efforts to justify and perpetuate it, they turn, without acknowledging the contradiction, to the argument of the universal presence of war in the animal kingdom. This urge to see in the world about us a universal warring instinct with which to justify our aggressive follies has acquired in our times a pretentiously pseudo-objective and pseudo-scientific aspect. Even the most elementary sampling of public opinion shows how deeply human beings have been conditioned to hold vague prejudices concerning the inevitability of strife, and the impossibility of controlling instincts supposedly inherited from a prehuman ancestral past.

The truth is that war is far from universal. In many societies it is completely unknown. According to the British anthropologist Hobhouse and his collaborators, among others the Australian aborigines, the Eskimos, the Ceylonese Veda, and the so-called Hottentots of South Africa know nothing of war. With regard to the Eskimos, confirmation is provided by the Arctic explorer Nansen, who cites an Eskimo letter of the year 1756. The letter's author cannot understand how men of the same faith hunt each other as if they were seals and steal the belongings of people they have never seen or known before. The fight for territorial possessions seems to him an unthought-of kind of greed with no attenuating explanation. He is surprised that the Europeans had not learned better manners among the Eskimos, and proposed sending witch doctors and missionaries to teach them the Eskimo way of life.

The association, so characteristic of American society, between masculinity and aggressiveness, is another culturally induced value that some have mistaken for a universal law. Among the Arapesh, one of the three tribes of New Guinea featured in Margaret Mead's classic study of sex roles, a man would be honored whom we, because of our historically limited concerns, would call "maternal" in his parental aspect and "feminine" in his sexual aspect. Arapesh men, just like the women, are brought up to be cooperative, unaggressive persons always ready to respond to the needs and demands of others. There is no trace among them of the idea that sex might be a powerful impelling force either for men or for women. In contrast to this, among the Mundugumor, another of the tribes studied by Mead, both men and women pride themselves on being aggressive, with all the aspects of personality related to maternal love reduced to a minimum of expression, and those related to sexual love raised to a maximum. Both men and women approximate a type of personality which we from within our Western culture would associate with a very violent and undisciplined man. Neither the Arapesh nor the Mundugumor maintain any contrast between the sexes: the Arapesh ideal is a gentle, sensitive man married to an equally gentle and sensitive woman, while the ideal of the Mundugumor is a violent, aggressive man married to a violent, aggressive woman. In the third tribe, the Tchambuli, Mead encountered the true reverse of the sexual attitudes of Western culture; the woman was dominant, impersonal, and managing while the man was emotionally subordinated and less responsible.[3]

The majority of writers agree that warfare, properly

speaking, does not seem to have existed before the Neolithic Age. In other words, war as an institution is less than ten thousand years old. It is true that evidence of human aggression goes back much farther. Thus Livingston points out that the remains of Sinanthropus, found near Peking some five hundred thousand years old, show signs of having suffered blows on the head.[4] Other such examples could be quoted.[5] But they are of little relevance here since all evidence of organized warfare is relatively recent. Warfare, in short, has had to evolve with culture; it did not spring out of nothing, and its origins are, of course, in those struggles of the more or less distant past to which the prehistoric remains of man's ancestors bear witness. But here we are interested not in more or less personal struggles but in rationalized, intraspecific aggression of numerically significant human groups.

Of course, there is no lack of violent death among the so-called primitive peoples. Chagnon reveals that twenty-four percent of adult men among the Yanomamö of Southern Venezuela die in conflicts, and the figure may be low.[6] Livingston quotes numerous similar cases. But such peoples, today and in the past, fight or fought in a different manner and for reasons different from the ones used to rationalize warfare among "civilized" people. For instance, there are many warrior societies in which a man is not in a position to take a wife until he has proved he has killed another man. Scalphunting among North American Indians, headhunting and tattooing among the Dyaks of

Borneo, perhaps even head-shrinking as originally carried on among certain Amazonian tribes, are other examples of warlike behavior intended to demonstrate manhood.

At more highly developed cultural levels we often find a warrior class, maintained by the economically productive segment of the population. According to certain authorities, the military role in such societies merges with the sacerdotal role even in times of peace. Thus in some feudal European societies, military service among the upper classes began with the stripping of the neophyte, who then attired himself in new garments in a ceremony analogous to admission into a religious order. With regard to existing war histories and war literature in general, it must not be forgotten that these works have always tended to reflect the values of the governing class that wields military command. Individual soldiers of genius and good fortune have been genuinely popular figures, and ordinary people have enjoyed hearing of their heroic deeds. But this kind of hero-worship is far from the glorification of war as such, which is an aristocratic trait. If history books seem to be full of nothing but wars, this may be because wars are easier to write about than other kinds of events, as well as more dramatic. As late as the Napoleonic period, most wars, however frightful for the combatants, were events of strictly local impact; news traveled slowly, and so did armies. A picture of the past as one of constant and universal belligerency is a complete distortion of the social reality.

Did war originate, then, in the heroic values of the warrior caste? It is true that the sacred aspect of warfare has survived up to our own times in one form or another. Thus a recent German author affirms: "War is the most solemn form of contact between peoples . . . it is necessary that wars should occur periodically because they reveal the will of nature so that it may recover its rights over those great human collectivities which attempt to remove themselves from its influence." From the *Iliad* and the *Odyssey* to the medieval and Renaissance romances of chivalry, from eighteenth- and nineteenth-century opera to present-day movies and television, the hero is obliged to pass a series of tests of his martial valor, at times joyfully and lightheartedly and at others, especially in the case of German poetry and romance, tearfully. The message of heroic literature is clear: to enjoy the embraces of his beloved, the hero must accept the embrace of war.

The outstanding recent exponent of this ethic is, without any doubt, the late Adolf Hitler, who always stressed that true manhood is to be won through war. "War is entirely natural, an everyday affair. War is eternal, animal. There is no beginning and there is no peace. All struggle is War." These characteristic phrases of his are clear examples of the erroneous social and biological concepts we intend to expose. All struggle is *not* war, if we adopt the reasonable definition of war as rationalized aggression between numerically significant groups of the same species. Even among those human groups who know nothing of war, such as the Greenlanders, struggle and conflicts do in fact exist. But they are centered on the kidnapping of women, who are valued not only sexually but economically. This is not a motive for which modern nations go to war.

Some authors have argued that war originated in the admiration those few evoke who have managed to enrich themselves notably and quickly by superior force of arms. But although examples of this kind are many, they do not explain the symbolic importance of war in most people's minds, since war is, after all, associated with self-sacrifice as well as with gain. It has also been pointed out that war, like sport or the cinema in recent times, has been used by rulers to distract the minds of the people. In this way rulers hope to manipulate power with greater tranquillity and acquire greater benefits from it. Machiavelli recommended such a use of war upon occasion; Hegel said that successful wars hinder domestic upheavals and strengthen the power of the state. The use to which certain dictators of the present day have put this principle is well known. But this kind of explanation makes warfare depend wholly on the will of one single individual or of a small group of individuals, which seems hardly credible.

It would seem rather that the warlike impulse possesses a collective character. This makes it necessary to seek its forms and origins elsewhere than in the conscious will or whim of a few. Whenever we find ourselves in the presence of a group, manifestations of aggression seem to become more regular and to participate in an unconscious automatism. Is the will to fight wars a product of collective motivation? Perhaps it once was; perhaps it still is, among the less developed peoples of the earth. But, despite what certain authors still maintain, most contemporary wars do not require the entire population to be mobilized, unless, of course, a population is being attacked by overwhelming force from without. Selective mobilization is a technological necessity, since modern armies are highly specialized, and a political asset, since in this way not too many people will question the reasons for the war. Once more, we must change the context of our inquiry.

PSYCHOANALYTIC EXPLANATIONS.

According to some psychoanalysts, the origin of political antagonisms may be found in the paranoiac mechanism by which each individual projects his interior "devil" upon the adversary. Another psychological mechanism cited in this connection is the universal tendency to self-punishment generally linked to residual guilt feelings. Self-punishment is perceived culturally as self-sacrifice, which is admired and encouraged. The military aspects of this are well expressed in the following words, attributed to an Italian general during the Second World War: "Casualty lists are the best propaganda . . . Every idea for which men have given their lives takes on a sacred and unquestionable character in the eyes of human beings."

The tendency toward self-sacrifice may also take the indirect form which some psychoanalysts have called the "Abraham complex," after the attempted sacrifice of Isaac by Abraham in *Genesis*. A military hierarchy is normally a gerontocracy, that is, a system in which the oldest have the most power. Those who direct the fortunes of war thus "consecrate" the best and healthiest of their sons to it. The culmination of such patriarchal power is to order the sacrifice of one's own son. This is always represented as a noble act. It is also an act that reinforces the authority of the military system, which, thanks to the progress of technology, is nowadays almost the only social medium in which the previous generation has power over youth. And the impact of technological progress on the military has been to lessen the value and prestige of accumulated experience as such.

In much the same way as the Abraham complex, psychoanalysis has suggested, the rite of circumcision symbolizes, among other things, the castration of the young. According to Allee parallel behavior may be observed amongst animals.

One psychological explanation of warfare that on the surface seems quite plausible is that it results from collective frustration. It is certainly possible to find frustrations in one nation that are more or less collective. But, under this theory, how can we account for the fact that they are not always conducive to war, or that when they are, they can be fantastic or senseless as well as serious?

AN EQUIVALENT TO WAR?

From the general psychological or even ethical point of view, we cannot overlook the fact that war brings enormous satisfaction to many human beings, as well as the opportunity to display high moral values. William James urged mankind to find a "moral equivalent to war." If we are going to take up this quest, we must give careful attention to the types of satisfaction that war supplies. One of these is most certainly an increased feeling of identity with others. Social research on human reactions to natural disaster has shown that, in the face of ominous threat, human beings become closely united. All distinctions, whether they be of class, age, or position tend to disappear, in a manner that seldom occurs in daily life. The same tends to be true of war. The presence of an enemy provides an unrivaled opportunity to discover our neighbors, to cross the barriers of class, education and belief that generally keep us divided, and that become operative again when danger no longer threatens. Under extreme tension our capacity to identify with our companions is increased. This enlarged concept of companionship, of group identity, brings with it a diminished sense of individual responsibility.

Every psychiatrist who has dealt with returned veterans has seen cases of individuals who could no longer function under the stress of peace because they were incapable of assuming responsibility or of making decisions that, during the war, had been made for them by others. In a democratic society we tend to assume that every adult individual is capable of independence and of making reasonable decisions. Nevertheless, during wars there are always a great many individuals who are thankful that the obligation of conscious selection has been removed. They prefer to submerge their individuality in the anonymity of the crowd, receiving orders from their superiors. For many, relief from immediate anxiety about everyday needs such as food and clothing more than compensates for the loss of liberty. This relief is not restricted to the weak or the neurotic. Making decisions is everyone's concern; that is why we readily give such large economic compensation to those who do make the important decisions within our society. War simplifies life for everyone: a collective decision must be made to vanquish the enemy, and all that follows depends on this. People who have difficulty in finding a fundamental purpose in life and who are dissatisfied with the mundane incentives that motivate the bulk of the population, encounter an almost religious satisfaction in dedicating themselves to an impersonal principle. They find fulfillment in submission, with victory as the only end in times of war.

The psychological advantages of group solidarity, the shedding of personal responsibility, and the incentive provided by a collective purpose are all worthy of further discussion. But here we are dealing solely with aggression. There is little doubt that, in the past, an important function of war was that it presented an apparently legitimate occasion to direct all of one's aggressive impulses toward an external object. The French sociologists Durkheim and Halbwachs, in their classic studies of suicide rates, proved that during wartime the rate among those not involved in combat fell off, on the average, by two-thirds of what it was during peacetime. Although there is no direct proof, it is hard not to conclude that among potentially suicidal persons war provides an outlet for aggressive tendencies that would otherwise have been directed inwards, at themselves. In other words, to the desperately unhappy war comes as a welcome release.

PEACE THROUGH WAR?

War is so deeply rooted in the spirit of nations that peace has nearly always been conceived as something established through warfare. Thus, the *pax Romana*—"the unbroken majesty of the Roman peace," as Gibbon called it—is only one manifestation of the idea of a peace that is imposed throughout the world by a power stronger, rather than more "peaceful" than all other powers. That such peace is no more than a different form of warfare has been amply demonstrated. It was during the *pax Romana* that slave mortality reached its peak. Pacification of this kind benefits only the pacifiers. The Aztec peace decimated the surrounding population. Conquering empires, from Alexander and Genghis Khan up to the present, have brought peace only at the price of slaughter. The colonial powers of the nineteenth century also used peace as a pretext for aggression; nobody can be unaware of the fact that Britain "pacified" India just as France "pacified" Morocco, Tunis and Algeria. The thesis of peace through war is still defended today by those who believe that only absolute control exercised by a great power can, by unifying the world, insure peace. Even if we neglect the point that apologists for this view are usually, by a remarkable coincidence, citizens of the proposed "pacifying power," the efficacy of the system has yet to be demonstrated. And even if it were, there would remain the question of whether such a peace is worth the loss of liberty.

CIVIL WAR AND INTERNATIONAL WAR.

If wars of pacification are nothing but self-interested exercises in brutality, internal wars are positive blood-baths. Among relatively recent conflicts, those with the highest casualty rates are the Thirty Years' War and the French Wars of Religion. In the nineteenth century the American Civil War caused far greater human losses than the Franco-Prussian War of 1870. The Paris Commune, again an internal conflict without imperialist or peaceful pretensions, also produced more victims than the Franco-Prussian War. More Russians died in the Russian Revolution than in the First World War, in which Russia was a major participant. The Spanish Civil War and the Chinese Revolution provide further examples of high mortality in more or less internal conflicts.

It is difficult, however, to be too impressed by the

distinctions between civil war, international war without imperialist or pacificatory motives, and warfare which, though employing different methods and techniques, reminds us of the situation under the *pax Romana.* Is this due to the fact that we are incapable of viewing the history of our own times objectively? Or do we stand in the presence of new social processes that only the hardened sociologist can describe and analyze? Whatever the reason, there is one thing of which, as anthropologists, we are quite certain: the reasoned and systematic extermination of human beings by other human beings is a biological absurdity.

NOTES

1. Quincy Wright, *A Study of War* (Chicago, 1942).

2. Robert Ardrey, *The Territorial Imperative: A Personal Inquiry into the Animal Origins of Property and Nations* (New York, 1966). For a refutation of Ardrey's views on numerous points see M.F. Ashley Montagu (ed.), *Man and Aggression* (New York and London, 1968), especially the article by J.P. Scott. Attempts to prove that early man was inherently aggressive have so far not succeeded. See Marilyn Keyes Roper, "A Survey of the Evidence for Intrahuman Killing in the Pleistocene," *Current Anthropology,* 1969. There is, in fact, no such evidence.

3. Margaret Mead, *Sex and Temperament in Three Primitive Societies* (New York, 1935).

4. Frank B. Livingstone, "The Effects of Warfare on the Biology of the Human Species," *Natural History,* 1967.

5. For example, the remains of a pelvis, run through by a spear, found on Mount Carmel, Israel, and dating back some 40,000 years. In the Western Hemisphere, there are the cracked human bones in the Coxcatlan cave, Tehuacan Valley, Mexico.

6. Napoleon A. Chagnon, "Yanomamö Social Organization and Warfare," *Natural History,* 1967.

7. W.C. Allee, *The Social Life of Animals* (New York, 1938).

2

STRENGTH AND SURVIVAL

It is often argued—and not least by the man in the street—that an inexorable law of nature will always prevent us from living in peace with one another. Pressed to identify this law, people will talk of "the survival of the fittest" as the method by which life eliminates the weak and so ensures the production of superior types. Although this idea is as old as man himself, the authority most generally evoked for it is Charles Darwin's theory of evolution.

In his day Darwin was excessively admired by some and savagely attacked and ridiculed by others. In 1859 the first edition—1,250 copies—of his master work, *The Origin of the Species by Natural Selection,* was sold out in twenty-four hours. It was, in point of fact, a serious book, scientifically organized and boring to the average reader, and in it the author showed extreme restraint. The only words that referred to the human species were those in the famous sixth edition (1872), where Darwin expressed his confidence that in the future "new light will be thrown on the origin of man and his history."

But the public was not deluded, and even before the publication of the book an intense interest had been aroused, due to the revolutionary implications of Darwin's theories. In spite of some previous explorations, it can be said that for the first time a scientific and soundly based theory had been advanced to explain the animal nature of man and reconstruct along general lines his possible origin. This was one more step, and perhaps the most important one, in the ceaseless search to discover the little corner which mankind occupies in space and time. Humanity has always refused to accept such an image of itself. It persecuted Copernicus and Galileo, and even burned Giordano Bruno in order to defend its conviction that the world which it inhabits is the center of the universe. Man has always opposed any theories which make him a subordinate in the order of things, or any laws which he himself does not administer and which lower him to the level of other living creatures. When the theory of evolution came into general knowledge, the arguments were less bloodthirsty but no less violent. In July, 1860, the eminent mathematician Samuel Wilberforce, Bishop of Oxford, challenged Thomas Henry Huxley, the Darwinian biologist, to a public debate. In sedate England, and in the most respectable academic surroundings, he told him sarcastically, "I should like to know if you are descended from monkeys on your grandfather's or your grandmother's side." To which Huxley replied with a pungent phrase (other versions of it exist, but the essential point is the same): "I would rather be descended from a hundred thousand monkeys than be related to a man who uses his great intelligence to obscure the truth."

Other stories about the reception of Darwin's ideas are more humorous, but reflect the same indignation at being classed with the animals. For instance, it is said that after attending a lecture on evolution, a British lady of society remarked: "If we really descended from monkeys, at least it should be kept from the lower classes." This would have found an apt retort in another remark, attributed to the anatomist G.W. Corner: "Do not worry, madam; after all, even if we are monkeys, we are the only monkeys who worry constantly about what kind of monkeys we are." When Darwin was awarded his doctorate *honoris causa* by the University of Cambridge in 1877, academic recognition had still not been able to calm the passions of his detractors; the students failed to respect the solemnity of the academic surroundings, something unheard-of at Cambridge up to that time. At the most solemn moment of the ceremony, a stuffed monkey was lowered from the gallery at the end of a rope, together with a metal hoop symbolizing the "missing link," which was followed by a student dressed in cap and gown.

But the most surprising thing is perhaps that this

outraged reaction has been carried over into the twentieth century. Even as late as 1925, in the state of Tennessee, a teacher was fined for teaching the theory of evolution.[1] In Britain an antievolution society still exists, and publishes books on the subject. The 1954 edition of the ten-volume *Universal History* published in Spain by Espasa-Calpe contains the statement: "No one believes today that man has descended from an extinct animal ancestor" (Vol. 1, p. 101).

But it is also true that from the very beginning of the debate on the theory of evolution more serious and scientific criticisms have been voiced. Darwin, naturally, could not explain everything: in the first place, the genetic aspects of the new biology were unknown. Darwin also suffered from his admirers; his biological ideas were rapidly generalized and exaggerated, not only by other biologists, but by many sociologists and philosophers. A social and philosophical Darwinism emerged, based on the concept of what Darwin had called "the struggle for existence." This struggle was thought to be the principal moving power in a grand and universal selective process in which the weak were destined to perish and the strong to survive. "Nature," said Thomas H. Huxley, Darwin's great associate, "operates like a gladiatorial combat in which the spectator does not even have to turn his thumbs down, since mercy is unknown." This concept is hardly an example of the detached scientific approach, and it may be suggested that the error consisted not in visualizing man as an animal, but in imagining that animals behaved like men. Darwin and Spencer lived at a time when modern industry was just being born; the competition then taking place between the rich, as well as between rich and poor, inclined them to believe that all nature was the same as the society that surrounded them. Colonial conquests, with their elimination of certain social forms and the substitution of others believed to be more 'advanced'; the spectacles afforded by the stock market; police brutality in the subjugation of the masses; the elimination of smaller businesses by great monopolies or through fluctuations in the business cycle—all these called to mind the world of Herbert Spencer or of Thomas H. Huxley, but not the real world of nature. It is hardly remarkable, then, that many of the most fervent propagandists of social Darwinism were not naturalists, or even philosophers, but businessmen like John D. Rockefeller, who once said: "The growth of a big business is nothing more than the survival of the fittest . . . it is truly the application of a law of Nature and of God's law."

This dramatic vision of nature had profoundly influenced the opinions of the layman. The concept of "the fittest," which is essential to Darwin's theory, is generally taken, though inexactly to mean "the strongest," from which it tends imperceptibly to become equivalent to "the most astute." It is easy to understand how this line of reasoning, expressed in an impersonal and scientific way, quietly transmuted the triumph of the stronger into the rights of the stronger. Darwin himself believed that some human races are superior to others: in *The Descent of Man* (1871) he compares skull types of different races and concludes that Englishmen are superior to Turks, and Saxons to Celts. Herbert Spencer, in his *Principles of Sociology* (1876-1896), held that throughout the history of man a preliminary barbaric stage was needed to eliminate both the weaker societies and the weaker members of the stronger societies. This could be achieved only through warfare. But in his zeal to justify the "natural" superiority of his own civilization, Spencer found himself obliged to recognize that "civilized" war tends to expose to death the stronger, "superior" elements while reserving the "physically inferior types" for reproduction. It did not occur to Spencer that his theory might be an oversimplification, so he concluded that war would "naturally" tend to disappear from the civilized world. Unfortunately, his prophecies were as bad as the reasoning on which they were based. Walter Bagehot, who was one of the first to apply Darwin's theories to society, followed a similar line of thought in his *Physics and Politics* (1872), which commanded great respect in its time. Ludwig Gumplowicz, in his *Outlines of Sociology* (1885) and many other works, carried Darwin's ideas to extremes in postulating an unbridgeable hostility between races, due to their different genetic stocks; some have seen him as an intellectual ancestor of Nazism. One of the few who rejected this narrow viewpoint at the time was the Russian Yakov Novicov who, in his attack on the French historian Ernest Renan—who also followed the line of social Darwinism—objected that not all forms of struggle were of equal social value.

We should not blame Darwin for all this. His ideas served the purpose of giving a scientific basis to certain national and class prejudices, and to Victorian man's general need for self-justification. They quickly became an almost religious dogma to his contemporaries. As scientific theories, their contribution is undeniable, but also, as is only natural in science, they need to be modified and partly reevaluated in the light of subsequent investigations. No one should doubt that the theory of evolution itself is subject to evolution. In scientific and academic circles these reassessments have continued to be made. But the "religion" of evolution lives on.

NATURAL SELECTION

What was it that Darwin actually discovered? It was that among all animals there is a selective process, similar to the one deliberately followed by stockbreeders, which he called "natural selection." Through this process gradual changes are produced in the different living species, like the ones breeders have achieved in domestic animals. The process undoubtedly takes place; to those brought up on the idea that each species had issued immutable and eternal from the hand of the Creator, this was a shocking fact. But, in describing the actual mechanisms of natural selection, Darwin, and to a greater extent his followers, placed exclusive emphasis on the part played by competition and struggle, neglecting cooperation and mutual aid, as though the survival of the fittest is always the result of the victory of the strongest, and the elimination of the unfit, the defeat of the weakest at the hands of the strong.

Actually, as we know since the rediscovery in 1900 of Mendel's great experiments, genetic selection proceeds far more subtly. In the first place, it makes sense to talk of genetic selection *only* when referring to a group that has been crossbred; to apply it at the individual level is an absurdity. Survival, in a genetic and evolutionary sense, always refers to the survival of the species or of definite characteristics within the species, and never to the survival of an individual member. Accordingly, if the phrase "survival of the fittest" has any meaning, it must apply to the fittest to procreate. Since the fittest, in this sense, are not necessarily the strongest, but only the best adjusted, and since the environment to which living things must adjust is subject to all kinds of changes, it is frequently impossible to predict who the fittest will be. Often, they will be the most adaptable. It is not uncommon that the very types considered least "perfect," or in other words, the ones which have failed to develop certain of their traits but which have retained others of a kind for which evolution so far has apparently found no use, may eventually emerge as the fittest to adjust to a drastic change in the environment.

Moreover, the environment to which the living being must adjust if he is to survive is a far cry from the uncomplicated reality imagined by those who believe in the "struggle for existence." In reality the environment is extremely complicated; it includes everything that surrounds the living being, including his own species, and in many cases it is hard to establish the boundaries between it and the individual exposed to it. Nature maintains a vast and complex balance among her countless living things, each of which constitutes part of the environment for all the rest; there is also a balance between these living forms and the inanimate world they inhabit. To adjust to the environment, under these conditions, is more a matter of cooperation than of dominance. If the idea of struggle had any scientific meaning in genetics, it would probably mean that a living being which struggles with its environment, including other living beings, is a freak doomed to prompt extinction.

Similarly, the mutations in the genes themselves that are most likely to persist are those which not only help the species to adjust to the environment but also stand in harmonious relation to the complex characteristics already fixed through the evolutionary process. In the same group of mutually fertile individuals, genetic selection may work not only to insure the survival of the strongest, but also that of other, weaker types of individuals. This is all in the interests of the group's adaptability. Perfect adjustment to the demands of the current environment would imply a degree of specialization so high as to endanger the group's survival should the environment suddenly change. Some species have actually reached this dangerous level of adjustment. Thus the rhinoceros, an animal well equipped to fight, is far more exposed to disappearance as a species than neighboring species which are less highly specialized, but are also less dependent upon specific ecological conditions. Survival under changed conditions can be assured only by the great diversity of traits which different individuals contribute to the common "genetic pool." This diversity presupposes among other things not only the preservation of "the strong," in the dubious language of the social Darwinists, but also of "the weak" and of all the intermediate types. This does not mean that "strength" is undefinable, but only that any given trait will in the end be harmful to the species if it is not combined with other traits. Otherwise we would find ourselves faced with Spencer's paradox regarding the death in war of the highest types: natural selection working in reverse. And yet wars continue, which inspired the biologist Neel to say ironically that if the strong devoted themselves to combat, the weak would inherit, if not the earth, at least the widows of the strong.

NOTE

1. John T. Scopes, the prosecuted teacher, was prevented by a technicality from appealing to the Supreme Court, and was forced to leave the teaching profession. (He later made a successful career in business.) A similar law in Arkansas was not declared unconstitutional by the Court until 1968.

3

AGGRESSIVENESS AND SURVIVAL AMONG ANIMALS

Observation of animal behavior has all too often been colored by exaggeration and bias. The idea that the jungle, in particular, is a scene of unrelieved ruthlessness is more of a romantic image than a scientific observation. According to Marston Bates, who studied jungle life at firsthand, the different species manage to coexist and perpetuate themselves without being dominated by any one plant or animal.[1] The shopworn metaphor of "the asphalt jungle" should be interpreted in a reverse sense: the jungle appears cruel and bloody exactly at those points where it most closely resembles the city. The first investigations of the behavior of the higher animals were almost invariably carried out with captive animals. But recently various investigators (Carpenter, Goodall, Harlow, Scott, Schaller, De Vore,

Lorenz, and others) have undertaken observation under natural conditions with entirely different results.

Aside from predatory hunting, which cannot be classed as strife or even as aggression, animals are much less belligerent in the wild than is usually imagined. Combat between animals of the same species is highly ritualized and is seldom mortal or even dangerous.

Aggressiveness between animals of the same species is generally linked to two related factors: territory and procreation. Territory may be at times a source of food, but it is above all an "opportunity to procreate."[2] Many birds, in the mating season, mark out territory in which to build their nests and lay in stocks of food; in this way they assure the survival of their progeny. During this time, the males of any species are extremely aggressive toward each other in defense of their territory. Thus the song of the nightingale or of the wild pigeon is probably not a paean of joy, but more probably a cry of warning or menace to possible invaders. Many fish also mark out a territory during the spawning season; nearly all carnivores do the same.

Aggressiveness within the species is generally sex-linked: in most animals the male is generally the more aggressive and is also the dominant sex (though female dominance does occur, especially among rodents and among birds). Studies have shown some relationship between the degree of aggressiveness and the male hormones. But this relationship is not as simple or as direct as might be imagined. Though it is true that the aggressiveness of the male increases as the quantity of male hormones increases, the females, in cases where they are dominant and more aggressive, do not seem to be affected in their behavior by either male or female hormones, and when they are not aggressive, they do not become so when supplied with male hormones. All this makes it hard to justify a clear universal law which would relate aggressiveness to virility.

On the other hand, animal competition for the female is a phenomenon that seems to have stimulated the imagination of many investigators at the expense of their sense of objectivity. Under natural conditions this competition is characterized by many exceptions and variations. Among red deer, fallow deer, and elk, in the rutting season, the buck who wins a butting contest takes over a group of females and procreates with all of them. This proves so exhausting that the male is able to preserve his dominance for only a short while before being forced to yield it to a fresh contender. Sheep follow a similar pattern of conduct, as do some other higher animals, including a number of primates: howling monkeys, for instance, tolerantly permit the females to change back and forth when two groups meet.

Still, it is undeniable that at times fights occur between animals of the same species. But when this happens, conditions are such that a fight to the death is avoided. The combat is generally a symbolic ritual. At times it is reduced to an exhibition, more like a dance than a fight, of the most terrible or imposing physical attributes of the rivals. Many carnivores, once the physical superiority of their foe has been established, fall over on their backs in an abject attitude, exposing the most vulnerable parts of their bodies. It would be easy for the victor to kill his defeated opponent at that moment. No doubt that is what he would do if he were a human being. But among these fierce hunters (including wolves) this does not happen. Similar behavior is observed among lizards. When two males of the *lacerta agilis* species fight, they first take a parallel stand and face in opposite directions. After a show of size and color, presumably designed to impress, each lizard turns his head and offers the enemy his occiput, the most protected part of his body, to be bitten. Generally the weaker bites first, in an effort to shake his opponent. If he fails, usually the weaker abandons the struggle and adopts a submissive attitude without waiting to be bitten. No biologist who has studied these animals has ever reported observing them biting each other in any other part except the occiput. The species *lacerta strigata major* follow a similar pattern, although they bite a joint instead of the occiput. Examples of this type of behavior can be found in very many different species, from birds and fishes to mammals such as the wolf, the reindeer, and the gorilla.

It would seem, then, that there is a strong inhibition in practically all the animal species that forbids the victor to kill his defeated rival. In this respect, man seems to be the oustanding exception. Thus, despite his position as the world's dominant species, he finds himself

46

in a potentially precarious situation. From the point of view of natural selection, while the interests of the *individual* might demand an unchecked aggressiveness (in order to eliminate all competitors for territory and for possession of the females), the interests of the *species* do not. As we have seen, natural selection favors the survival of those species which have established behavior patterns that exclude indiscriminate butchery. It should now be obvious how oversimplified are the popular ideas on this subject. If the principle that selection favors the survival of the fittest is still basically valid, it is so hard to apply in practice that its opposite—survival of the least fitted—is true at least some of the time. If "the weak" and "the strong" possessed any clear scientific meaning, it could be argued that *exclusive* survival of the strong would result in something like the well-known phenomenon of the degeneration of families in which intermarriage of closely related persons is the rule. Because natural selection needs a broad field in which to operate, unless "strong" families renew their genetic heritage with fresh additions from "weak" genetic stocks, they degenerate.[3]

Neither the laws of natural selection, when properly understood, nor the observed behavior of individuals among the other animal species yield any explanation or justification of our own bellicose behavior. Even territoriality, though a deeply rooted instinct in so many species, is not stronger than the instinct of self-preservation. Furthermore, concern with territory varies according to species. Some groups are almost exclusive;

others share a common territory in harmony with others of the same species or with other species; fishing birds which live in huge colonies seem to share fishing rights over a wide expanse of sea, which becomes a sort of communal territory.[4] In short, the distribution of territories under natural conditions hardly resembles the romantic concept of a ruthless jungle. Animals defend their territory only against males of the same species, or of a species with the same needs for food and procreation; they will share their territory peaceably with thousands of other living creatures. An extensive territory "belonging" to a large carnivore, such as a tiger, is at the same time occupied by many small rodents, for example, and the lesser territories of each of these by other, smaller organisms. Finally, territoriality seems closely linked to the mating season, something that human beings do not have. In fact, man is the only animal that lacks a mating season; certain animals, such as the anthropoids, which were also believed to lack one, now appear to have an attenuated form of it.

But how valid is this kind of comparison in any case? Can it not be argued that human behavior, because of man's immensely more complex social development, cannot be compared with that of animals at all? But modern research has shown that the social life of animals is far more complex than anyone had suspected. Many animals live in actual communities, which shows that social life emerged at a very early stage in the process of evolution. For instance, if we observe a chicken yard we find that the hens peck each other frequently but not indiscriminately; there is a pyramidal social order from the hen at the top, which pecks all the rest and is pecked by none, to the ones at the bottom, which are pecked by all the rest without pecking any in return. This is known to naturalists as "the pecking order." This same order probably exists among other animals which live together in groups. It is not difficult to find a parallel in human society, where the "pecks" are usually only verbal or symbolic.

The pecking order is established apparently through more or less formalized but never mortal conflicts in which animals engage on achieving maturity or on coming into contact with each other for the first time. Frequently the social order is firmly established by the first series of conflicts, which are not repeated even if they were only of a ritual nature. In other cases the conflicts are repeated from time to time, and the social order may be reorganized; in others, competition is observed only during the mating season. In this order of dominance, the dominant animals enjoy priorities for feeding and procreation. Here is an undoubted example of a selective mechanism, but it has not been possible to establish a clearcut relationship between dominance and strength or any other special qualification. Among the anthropoids, whose social scales are more complex, an animal which is not dominant, but which possesses some special attribute, will perhaps under special circumstances exercise authority over the group (such as choosing the line of march). But this is debatable. Neither can an invariable relationship between dominance and sex be established. Although usually the males dominate the females, there are exceptions, as among certain kinds of sparrows, where the females dominate; the same occurs with some small mammals, like hamsters. In some bird species, dominance is independent of sex, and in others it shifts according to different phases of the life cycle. Is the pecking order a clear and direct application, though not a deadly one, of the struggle for existence? According to Roger Brown, the evidence is far from conclusive.

A sense of the need for a dominant order to insure individual survival does not seem to be clearly established in the animal world. On the other hand, such an order can be said to have value for the survival of the group and the species. In fact, these social structures and ritualized relations between individuals tend to prevent mortal combat and give cohesion to the group. Thus, Wynne-Edwards believes that the dominant order is not really a device for selection on the individual level, but that it operates mainly to insure survival of the group.[5] He calls it "the social guillotine," and relates it to the homeostatic theory of social groups. According to this theory, in animal groups a balance is maintained between the amount of food available and the number of members. Territoriality and the order of dominance contribute to this state of balance by discouraging the reproduction of a number of animals whose offspring might cause the population density to increase out of proportion to the available food supplies. But this "automatic birth control" is accomplished without strife, without killings, without war. Wynne-Edwards compares this process with the predicament of three men afloat on a raft with only sufficient food for two. The "homeostatic" solution, according to him, does not consist in two of them murdering the other, not even in order to eat his flesh, but in the third man's voluntary disappearance. In the mechanics of natural selection, this decision of the individual is replaced by a supposed group decision, but the results are the same—to assure the survival of the group without murdering some of its members. However, the choice of the individuals who must disappear does not appear to have any connection with their supposed "inferiority," whether as to strength, adaptability, or any other quality.

Imagine the whole of mankind as passengers on a sinking ship; in order for the species to survive, the main thing is that an accepted convention shall be in force which decrees that only as many people take to the lifeboats as there is room for, and that the rest renounce all chance for rescue. It is of no importance —within certain obvious limits—who these self-sacrificing heroes are; once the filling of the boats to capacity is assured, the personal qualities of the passengers are of secondary importance. Thus in Noah's Ark it would have been disastrous to waste time choosing from each species the best pair, or the most fit, especially since it could not have been foreseen for what conditions the specimens chosen would have to be best or most fit when the Flood was over. Trying to select the best of a species in an absolute sense is anything but natural, and man is the only being capable of imagining such a thing.

What happens to animal aggressiveness within these more or less carefully regulated animal societies? According to Brown, fighting for food between animals *of the same species* is almost unknown. When two groups of chimpanzees meet, they do not fight. This is a special case, but an interesting one nevertheless, in view of our very close links with the African anthropoids. The legendary gorilla is a peaceful animal under natural conditions; its sex life is extraordinarily placid, and it is generally content to settle challenges to its domination with a menacing gesture. Among macaco monkeys the adult females are sometimes dominant. Other primates, such as baboons, are more aggressive, and establish their dominance by strife and frequent biting of each other. But they never fight to the death. In any case, sexual passion does not seem to play an essential role in primate societies, especially those which are known, because they most closely resemble man, as the "Big Four": gorillas, chimpanzees, orang-utans, and gibbons.

Scott, who has carefully studied the organization of some animal societies, found that the level of aggressiveness depended on the level of social disorganization within the group. In his experiments he placed together two different colonies of rats. He found that they fought only when (a) social disorganization (e.g., the mixing of two different rat colonies) was forcibly introduced; (b) escape was impossible. He concluded that strife is not the first but the last resort. Scott also lists three fundamental characteristics of struggle between animals: (1) as opposed to the sexual instinct and hunger, the primary stimulus for struggle is an external one; (2) this attitude is acquired through previous experience; (3) in vertebrates, this attitude is tied in with territoriality.[6]

The *acquired* nature of aggressiveness is important. Scott found that the habit of success in combat contributed to the aggressiveness of the rat in fights arranged in the laboratory, whereas by raising males among females, with whom struggle is not customary, he succeeded in developing in them a disinclination to quarrel. Thus habit and learning seem to be stronger than physiological instincts. In one experiment, a group of mice was artificially obliged to compete for food until they developed a habit of struggle, in the course of which they evolved an order of dominance; male hormones were then administered to the dominated mice, which promptly overthrew the leaders and made them subordinates. But when the hormones were withheld, the mice which had successfully revolted after taking them still continued to be dominant. In another experiment, a colony of mice trained for fighting was mixed in with another colony composed of peaceable mother mice, who then learned aggressive behavior from new arrivals.

Certain other experiments suggest that the behavior of cats toward mice is an acquired characteristic. A kitten which is raised in the company of mice is never impelled to attack them. It has been suggested that this, however, is a perversion of a natural instinct, since apparently cats not raised in the company of mice will pursue them on first sight without previous experience. In any case, it would seem that this involves an early and primary stage of learning, which has been called "imprinting." One of the outstanding students of imprinting is Konrad Lorenz. As part of a series of experiments, he succeeded in instilling unfamiliar conduct patterns in newly hatched goslings, substituting his own image for that of the mother, so that they followed him about as though he *were* their mother! They continued to do so even when a real female goose was provided as an alternate choice. The strength of these early impressions proved to be so strong that these geese, on attaining maturity, did not project their sexual impulses toward members of their own species, but toward human beings.[7] If conditioning of this nature can so deform an instinct, as in the example of the kittens raised with mice, we must conclude that there are limits on particular instincts, at least, and perhaps on all instincts. Still more recent studies indicate that so-called instincts may themselves be learned, at least in part. Thus the behavior of sea gull chicks seems to show that their feeding instinct is not fully developed at birth. In order to develop normally, the chick must have a certain kind of experience.[8]

In any case, animal social structures all seem to tend towards control of the instinct toward strife within the species. This is, to all appearances, the meaning of domination and territoriality. The great anthropoids—the "Big Four" already referred to—are territorial animals, and although we have already seen that territoriality has many aspects, more than might readily be imagined, it is logical to suppose that biologically man is probably a territorial animal. But even excluding the problem of the mating season, which is nonexistent in man and which seems closely linked to territoriality, consideration of all the different forms which early conditioning, or socialization, has superimposed on territoriality complicates the problem enormously.

Among domestic animals, territoriality adopts strange forms; it may even seem to be absent altogether. In sheep dogs, for instance, it has been completely eradicated by domestication. In other kinds of dogs, "territory" may symbolically consist of the master's affection. In any case it is obvious that the territory of domesticated dogs has nothing to do with a natural need for living space, or with the hunting instinct; the size and nature of the space that makes up their territory depend exclusively on the dictates of man. It would be hard to maintain that a lapdog protects the apartment where it lives because of its sex or hunting instincts. Some naturalists believe that the dog's habit of frequent urination has evolved from an instinct inherited from the past to mark off definite territory for its own recognition. Many animals do, in fact, resort to such a procedure or similar ones in the wild. But it is clear that in the case of the domesticated dog, the instinct is superfluous and even illogical. The dog arbitrarily marks off a territory, which he intends neither to use nor to defend: many other dogs will come and urinate in the same spot and be regarded with indifference. This purely symbolic establishment of rights without taking actual possession may be more like that of poets and lovers when they speak of "their" places in a sentimental sense. If this occurs among animals, it is logical to suppose that man, self-disciplined from the beginning, must have greatly developed his faculty for orienting his territorial "instinct" towards goals that have little to do with the instinct's original function.

We have reviewed some of the prejudices and misapprehensions which are in circulation regarding animal ferocity. It should also be pointed out that for a long time more attention was focused on this aspect of animal behavior than on its cooperative and social side. This tendency still persists in many minds. But researchers have found the facts to be otherwise. Scott, for instance, sees animal societies in general as highly cooperative. One investigator who has made a close study of wolves found that their outstanding characteristic is friendliness.[9] Among the primates we find abundant evidence of cooperation. Female baboons which have no offspring nurse the young of other females. The behavior of these females, who have been called "aunts" or "baby sitters," seems to have parallels among other primates. Thus gelade monkeys usually march along the edge of a precipice (which protects them from surprise attack), while on the unprotected side the males march to screen the females and the young. Among baboons, a mother with young evokes a more friendly attitude from companions of either sex; the males, particularly, adopt a protective attitude for several weeks after birth of the young. The habit that many kinds of monkeys have of picking each other clean of lice is considered by some naturalists as the most primitive example of affective behavior among animals.

Goodall has observed and filmed the behavior of chimpanzees which sit together, eat together and hunt together.[10] The shrill and frequent screams of these animals, interpreted by other investigators as examples of aggressiveness, according to this writer appear to be only expressions of pleasure on meeting. Nissen and Crawford studied the behavior of young and well-fed chimpanzees sharing their food; they found that such sharing may occur spontaneously, or it may be proceeded by a "request" for a share.[11] Crawford experimentally induced a much more complex cooperative pattern in chimpanzees. After training a number of them to obtain food through the operation, in sequence, of four devices marked with different colors, he placed bars between two of them, leaving each one able to manipulate two of the four devices; the correct sequence required a cooperation between the two on what we would consider a conscious level. In some cases the chimpanzees were able to cooperate successfully and obtain food.[12]

Surprising examples of cooperative behavior have been observed also among lower animals. Thus Lorenz describes what he calls "friendship" among geese: the males tend to form inseparable pairs, and even attempt copulation. When they find that this is impossible, they desist, without for that reason ending the friendship. When a female is present, she will gradually approach them and couple with one of them. These animals then perform a curious post-mating ceremony. But in this situation the male which has coupled addresses the ceremony to his friend and not to the female. Usually the female will later couple with the other male, and thus, little by little, sometimes after a year, a perfect triangle is established and the three will mutually address pre-coupling and post-coupling ceremonies to each other.[13]

The degree to which individual animals participate in social life has a strong influence on the development of their patterns of conduct, and even on what might be called their intelligence, or problem-solving capacity. Rats brought up alone require nearly twice as much time to learn to solve problems in the maze than those which have been raised in the company of other rats. They are also much more aggressive. Rhesus monkeys which are kept in isolation at an early age develop tendencies toward self-punishment and overly aggressive behavior. Participation in social life is even more important than life with the mother; monkeys which lived with a simulated mother made of terry cloth, but which played twenty minutes a day with three other monkeys of their own age, grew up with normal attitudes.

It is clear that natural selection works by adjusting different members of the same species to different environments. What the social Darwinists seem to have missed is that this process helps to *eliminate* competition within the species, since it provides for variations on the same type. Thus among the beaver, the old ones emigrate downstream and the young ones upstream. Survival depends on the degree of adjustment to an environment. This includes, it must be emphasized, *everything* that surrounds the living being, including fellow beings. Here, again, survival has been misinterpreted as survival of the fittest. Among mammals in general, as well as among primates, cooperation contributes more to survival than strife. The first step toward cooperation is copulation between male and female to preserve the species. This applies throughout the animal kingdom, and includes ourselves. Those who insist that men behave like wolves fail to make clear whether they refer to the behavior of wolves toward sheep, or of wolves toward other wolves. Wolves, after all, live in packs. A truly solitary animal is a rare phenomenon. Individuals of the same species depend on each other in various ways, and their relations may range from the most arduous competition to complete toleration, from casual to obligatory cooperation. The discipline imposed by nature impels us toward mutual assistance at least as frequently as toward warfare. The "fittest" may also be the friendliest.

NOTES

1. Marston Bates, *Where Winter Never Comes* (New York, 1952).

2. Roger Brown, *Social Psychology* (New York, 1965).

3. For a short but clear introduction to the theory of natural selection see Theodosius Dobzhansky, *Heredity and the Nature of Man* (New York, Signet Science Library Edition), pp. 127–32.

4. Brown, op. cit.

5. V.C. Wynne-Edwards, *Animal Dispersion in Relation to Social Behavior* (London, 1962).

6. J.P. Scott, *Aggression* (Chicago and London, 1958), and *Animal Behavior* (New York, 1963).

7. Konrad Lorenz, *On Aggression* (New York, 1963).

8. Jack P. Hailman, "How an Instinct Is Learned," *Scientific American,* 221, 98–106, 1969.

9. A. Murie, "The Wolves of Mt. McKinley," *U.S. Dept. of the Interior Fauna Series, No. 5* (Washington, D.C., 1944). See the discussion by E.M. Banks, D.H. Pimlott, and B.E. Ginsburg, "Ecology and Behavior of the Wolf," *American Zoologist,* 7, 220–381, 1967.

10. Jane Goodall, "Feeding Behavior of Wild Chim-

panzees," *Symposia of the Zoological Society of London, No. 10* (London, 1963), pp. 39–48.

11. A.W. Nissen and M.P. Crawford, "A Preliminary Study of Food Sharing Behavior in Young Chimpanzees," *Journal of Comparative Psychology,* 22, 383–419, 1936.

12. M.P. Crawford, "The Cooperative Solving of Problems by Young Chimpanzees," *Journal of Comparative Psychology,* 22, 383–419, 1939.

13. Lorenz, op. cit.

4

THE WARRIOR IMPULSE

Man is both a cultural and a biological being. Concentration on one of these aspects to the exclusion of the other makes it impossible to discover at what points culture and biology are mutually influenced. It is especially important to remember this as we turn to examine the explanations of human aggression that have been put forward by psychologists and psychoanalysts.

Some psychologists have studied human aggression with the same kinds of methods and criteria that are employed in the study of animal behavior. Scott, for example, applies a great part of his conclusions to both men and rats, since the essential features of conflict behavior appear to him to be found as much in one as in the other.[1] One proof of this similarity, he thinks, is to be found in the influence of social disorganization on aggression. A large part of conflict behavior and of human aggressiveness is, for him, poor adaptation, and can be explained as a result of frustration. For instance, crime statistics in the United States show that the majority of crimes can be attributed to persons under twenty-five years of age; there has even been a year when most of the lawbreakers proved to be less than eighteen years old. Scott argues that the lesson to be learned from these figures is that the majority of crimes are committed in an interval when a man is no longer under family control and generally has not yet formed his own family—in other words, the period of maximum family and social disorganization. Although Scott admits that certain hereditary behavior differences can be found, he insists that on the individual level, if sufficiently investigated, external factors are always present, and that in the majority of the cases, these factors amount to family disorganization. His investigations seem to demonstrate that aggression, in animals as well as in men, always does result from exterior stimuli, and that there is no proof of an interior stimulus—not, at any rate, one that could be called a true innate tendency toward aggression.

Recent work indicates that both fighting and defeat produce striking changes in both the levels of blood hormones and brain biochemistry. Such experiences also have effects upon the testes and accessory sex glands.

Some authors find no evidence for the existence of an 'aggression center.' Fighting between monkeys can be elicited only by noxious brain stimulation or external foot shock.

These results indicate the importance of the effect of training and experience upon aggressive behavior and raise the question of whether all aggressive behavior elicited by brain stimulation may simply be the result of pain or similar noxious stimulation.[2]

It must be admitted nevertheless that some physiological researchers, notably K.E. Moyer, believe aggressive behavior to be determined by a whole complex of factors, internal, external, and experimental. They reject the terms "aggressive drive" and "innate aggressiveness," referring instead to "internal physiological impulses to aggression."[3]

On the group level, social disorganization seems to stimulate aggression in men as well as in rats. For example, it can be argued that violence prevailed in the West of the United States during the very period in which immigrant groups were searching for stability and social organization. The final report of the United States Commission on the Causes and Prevention of Violence blames much unrest and violence on poor living conditions. Only by improving the quality of life in areas of high population density can this particular source of violence be eliminated. The notion that the existence of poverty-stricken ghettoes is somehow "natural" or biologically determined is too absurd to be worth discussion.

An important point made by many psychologists is that aggressiveness must be learned. Success obtained in aggressive situations tends to reinforce the propensity toward aggression; children can be brought up to be aggressive. There is much discussion on this point; some psychologists tend to see an instinct or an innate propensity, more or less latent, in human aggression. They cite, among other things, the apparent fact that aggression seems to reach its maximum potential during the early years of life. But other researchers have shown that it actually follows an S-curve; at the end of infancy it appears to decrease, and then in adolescence it is temporarily intensified.[4] The fact that men are generally more aggressive than women, and that this appears to be true independently of the influences of sex hormones, appears to support the thesis of innate propensity. But it is here that we enter the web where cultural and biological factors are hopelessly intermingled, and, as we shall see later, it is especially hard to separate them when studying the origins of human aggression.

Many ingenious experiments have been devised with a view to demonstrating that aggression depends directly upon feelings of frustration. In one of these experiments, each subject operated some buttons that, he was told, administered electrical discharges of varying intensity to another subject. The subject was instructed to "reward" or to "punish" another individual (who was secretly following the experimenter's instructions) according to his answers to certain problems. Both individuals were separated by a screen and, in reality, no discharges were produced; the individual who was supposed to be receiving the discharges merely behaved as if he were in pain. After the subject began to experience frustration, because nothing seemed to be happening as it was supposed to, his level of aggression, as measured by a dial that was supposed to show the intensity of the shock he was administering, increased to a marked degree.

In another series of experiments, the degree of constructiveness in children's games was examined. For example, some children were given incomplete toys. They played with them very contentedly until they were shown the missing parts. They were able to see these parts (a basin that went with a small boat, a little iron that corresponded to an ironing board, and so forth), but were not able to reach them. The children then displayed a marked tendency to resort to forms of play that corresponded to a mental age much lower than their true age, such as banging the table or scribbling instead of writing.[5]

Frustration is undoubtedly a weighty stimulus toward the freeing of aggressive conduct. Both Berkowitz[6] and Holloway,[7] however, demonstrate clearly that we are far from proving that all frustration is followed by aggression. On the contrary, we can prove that frustration is often followed by other forms of behavior. What is more, individual psychology—in this case, the psychology of individual frustration—cannot explain collective phenomena, such as warfare.

Other psychologists, approaching the problem from a clinical point of view, have come up with facts that, they argue, suggest that aggression is purely physiological in character. The suppression of certain zones of the cerebral cortex of a cat provokes uncontrollable and incongruous aggression; so does stimulation of certain glands. But since other surgical alterations can provoke reactions of extreme meekness, we can only conclude that aggression is no more "innate" than its opposite.

Psychoanalytic theory also tends to treat aggression as a primary instinct. Freud himself, in his earlier writings, gave great importance to this instinct, considering it to be one of the two fundamental ones, the other being the erotic instinct of pleasure. Later on he clarified his point of view and came to consider the aggressive instinct as derived, not fundamental. He now declared the two fundamental instincts to be those of life, or Eros, and of death, or Thanatos. The latter, which for the Freud of the early period was derived from the primary instinct of aggression, now became a primary instinct: life's tendency to stop and "rest." Many of Freud's disciples did not follow his ideas about the death instinct and some of them returned to his original theory of aggression, which they considered the orthodox one. This is probably the reason why many psychologists today allot great importance to aggression, which they consider to be innate and cosubstantial in the structure of the unconscious. They are opposed by another school, the so-called "cultural psychoanalysts," who appeal to the studies that have been made in combining psychoanalysis with ethnology. These studies seem to suggest that certain basic components of human personality depend upon cultural factors to a far greater extent than orthodox psychologists are willing to admit. The leading representative of this school is Margaret Mead.

We have, then, two opposing points of view in the psychological study of aggression. The first is that of Lorenz and Ardrey, who attempt to explain human aggression as due to an innate instinct, determined by genetic factors which reveal themselves independently of any learning processes. The second is that of Scott, who maintains that the primary stimulus for aggressive conduct is external, and that there is no form of internal stimulus that *necessarily* drives an individual to engage in struggle. Scott concludes, on the basis of comparative physiological studies of conflict behavior in a variety of animals, that the emotional and physiological factors involved in such behavior are entirely different from those implicit in sexual or other allegedly basic forms of behavior. Support for the second viewpoint has recently come from Holloway, who casts doubt upon the idea that man possesses any aggressive instinct at all. Holloway tells us that if we understand by "instinct" a pattern of fixed and invariable action directed toward an equally invariable and defined set of stimuli (and this is the usual sense of the term), there would appear to exist practically no example of this kind of instinct in man, let alone a specific instinct of aggression. If Holloway is right, this would be a fatal blow to the position of Lorenz and Ardrey. As for the orthodox psychoanalytic view of aggression, it is not even consistent with itself, for while it conceives aggression as an innate and primary biological instinct, it sets out to educate and finally dominate this supposedly ineluctable instinct through therapy. But whatever we conclude about these psychological studies of aggression, it must be admitted that they have so far contributed little to our understanding of peace and the threats to it. No self-respecting observer of animal behavior would ever try to explain the aggressive behavior of the members of one species towards each other merely by positing an innate aggressive tendency. Nevertheless, when we come to deal with human social behavior, we are always being told that we should be satisfied with this sort of explanation. For example, in a relatively recent symposium on aggression, a distinguished panel of contributors, whose fields range from ethology to social anthropology, conclude that human aggression is due to an aggressive instinct.[8] One of the projects at this symposium consisted mainly of an impressive exhibit showing the horrifying incidence of cruelty, sadism, and massacre throughout man's history. The author, Storr, concludes that only innate aggressiveness could explain these phenomena. The argument undoubtedly seems plausible. But by taking another group of historical examples it would be equally possible to infer the existence of innate tendencies toward cooperation, altruism, and self-sacrifice—or perhaps even to change in styles of clothing or of good looks. There are two fundamental reasons why this type of explanation is unsatisfactory. One is that it depends for its effect on endless repetition of the same point; it is more of a rhetorical device than a scientific demonstration. The other is that it is not based on detailed analysis of the conditions under which certain types of behavior will or will not occur—the only type of analysis that would permit us to make verifiable conjectures with regard to the causal factors that might be present. Even if it were true that hidden innate tendencies underlie the various forms of competition, conflict and cooperation, the complexity of man's social conduct is such that this type of explanation would not get us very far.

Just as unsatisfactory are the purely physiological explanations of aggression that reduce both it and all other forms of human behavior to an organic level. Thus R.F. Ewer[9] writes that "behavior is something which an animal has got in the same way as it may have horns, teeth, claws, or other structural features." I cannot agree; it seems to me that behavior is something very much more complicated. Physiology has a valuable contribution to make, but it defines aggression in too limited a manner to be capable of explaining it completely. Thus some physiologists speak of aggression as if it is some kind of electrical battery that, once charged, *needs* to be discharged—or even, as Peter H.

Klopfer has complained, as if it were "a fluid liable to seep through cracks in the cranium."[10] Experimental manipulation may produce violent or anti-social behavior in animals and humans. But such behavior is no more the product of "innate impulses" than the music of a piano sonata is "innate" in the piano. To quote Klopfer again, it is far more likely that "we 'contain' aggression about as much as a radio 'contains' the music we hear issuing from it." Without culture there would be no sonata and no radio program.

We must conclude, then, that investigations of man's aggressiveness *simply as a biological being* have only a limited value. They certainly cannot reveal to us the exact nature of the relation, supposing that one exists, between aggressiveness and war, or even between aggressiveness and other forms of hostility or negativity that exist among human beings. Indeed, given the power of modern weapons to destroy at a long distance from the human point of control, the people who actually fight wars need not be aggressive types at all.

Of course, Lorenz may well be quite correct when he asserts, for instance, that the behavior of the Indians of the North American prairies is notoriously aggressive due to selective factors that predispose them toward warfare. However, this in no way contributes to any explanation of the existence of warfare itself. A comparable example can be taken from the area of genetics. The sickle cell gene of malaria has a very high frequency in East Africa, where malaria is endemic. But this fact does not lead to the conclusion that the gene itself has enabled Africans to survive in this region in spite of the malaria. Actually, it can be shown that the presence of the gene has very little to do with the local population's chances of survival or of its rate of reproduction.

To return to the question of social disorganization, even if it does appear to have a similar effect on humans and on rats, the similarity ceases to be so clear when we give full consideration to the cultural element. In man, the diversity of *possible* reactions is infinitely greater— as great as the difference between man's varied culinary achievements and the rat's simple diet. For example, Dollard discovered that during the years of the catastrophic price drop in cotton, lynchings and attacks against Negroes increased in the southern states of the United States. This law, however, is not valid everywhere. When similar economic difficulties broke out in Brazil, political rather than racial conflicts resulted.[11]

But do we even know what the psychological studies really mean? Some psychologists have made the observation that in the majority of the studies on aggression, especially those on the hypothesis of aggression frustration, there is no clear distinction between aggression and hostility or even between aggression and any other negative attitude. Moreover, concepts such as hostility and negativity are not easily applicable to animals, nor are they readily defined in human beings. It is almost impossible to omit all moral considerations from descriptions of allegedly aggressive behavior; the very idea of abnormality that is always implicit in concepts such as hostility is a highly debatable one. Acts that are considered hostile and destructive by a bourgeois may appear highly constructive to the revolutionary who commits them. Christ's hostility toward the merchants in the temple cannot be equated with the aggressiveness of an animal exposed to certain stimuli, and is not to be described by the same methods.

Accordingly, if we are to study war and peace we must opt for the description of human behavior in terms of its significance in the world of human culture and human perceptions. In this way, we shall be forced to abandon explanations drawn from the realm of biology. But there is no reason to regret this. How can prejudice, ill will and contempt be explained biologically? A rat may attack another animal, but it will not scorn it, make fun of it, or consider it inferior. Above all, a rat cannot lie. How, then, can we be sure that human culture and human intelligence, which separate us from the animals, do not play as great a part in human aggression as any instincts that we may have inherited from our animal origins? This conclusion differs only in emphasis from that of Nikolaas Tinbergen, professor of animal behavior at Oxford University, whose pioneering experimental work has inspired views such as those of Desmond Morris in *The Naked Ape* (1967) and *The Human Zoo* (1969). Tinbergen has argued that human aggression results from the *cultural* reinforcement of a biological heritage that man shares with the animals. He thinks it possible that man may save himself from extinction by redirecting his aggressiveness into competitive activities other than war.[12] But why shouldn't culture reinforce other aspects of the biological heritage? We know far too little to assume that aggressiveness is the biological norm, even among animals. Indeed, Edward O. Wilson, professor of zoology at Harvard, goes so far as to suggest that "pacifism is the rule among animal species."[13]

It is the task of science to carry the search for causes as far back as it can. But we will learn very little about human warfare from studying the birds and the bees. A certain conditioned reflex—or rather, what remains of it today—may be admitted to exist in squids, apes, and human beings. But this does not mean that the total behavioral pattern of all three can be equated. Is Vietnamese nationalism a result of the "territorial imperative?" The question is idle. To keep on suggesting that human aggression has an innate biological cause is like insisting that our sensations of heat and cold are determined by mental fantasies, and that it makes no difference what we wear.

NOTES

1. J.P. Scott, *Aggression* (Chicago and London, 1958), and *Animal Behavior* (New York, 1963).
2. J.P. Scott and B.E. Eleftherion, in a symposium on "The Physiology of Fighting and Defeat," *Science,* 162, 935–6, 1968.

3. K.E. Moyer, "Internal Impulses to Aggression," *Transactions of the New York Academy of Sciences,* Series II, 31, 104–114.

4. Denis Hill, in J.D. Carthy and F.J. Ebling (eds.), *The Natural History of Aggression* (New York and London, 1964).

5. For these and similar experiments consult the inventory in Bernard Berelson and Gary A. Steiner, *Human Behavior* (New York, 1964).

6. Leonard Berkowitz, *Aggression* (New York, 1962).

7. R.L. Holloway, Jr., "Human Aggression," *Natural History,* 1967.

8. J.D. Carthy and F.J. Ebling (eds.), *The Natural History of Aggression* (New York and London, 1964).

9. R.F. Ewer, *The Ethology of Mammals* (New York, 1968).

10. Peter H. Klopfer, in *Science,* 165, p. 887, 1969.

11. As reported in Gaston Bouthoul, *Les guerres* (Paris, 1951), and in Berelson and Steiner, op. cit.

12. See especially his inaugural address at Oxford on "War and Peace in Animals and Man," reprinted by the journal *Science* in 1968.

13. *San Francisco Chronicle,* June 13, 1969, p. 8.

5

TWO KINDS OF EVOLUTION

The foregoing chapters have shown how distorted are the ideas accepted by public opinion concerning the supposed laws of nature (or of God, according to the elder John D. Rockefeller) that are generally referred to by the Darwinian terms "struggle for existence" and "natural selection." The truth is that most of us tend to flee from our responsibility for failing to achieve peace by blaming biological urges—urges that in other respects we are reluctant to recognize. The result is that in making comparisons between ourselves and other living things we falsely interpret their behavior and distort the facts. That these comparisons are false can be shown in many different ways. In fact, it is extremely doubtful whether "struggle," "fight," and "war" can be used as synonyms; the connection between them, if any, may be only a remote one.

IS PEACE INEVITABLE?

Biology cannot account for the persistence of warfare because most patterns of human conduct are not transmitted to successive generations by biological processes. Also, cultural evolution is so rapid, compared to biological evolution, that we cannot assume that *any* culture is in a state of static equilibrium. Although we can reasonably suppose that the human species exists because it has succeeded in adjusting to its environment, we cannot suppose that a culture exists for the same reason. All cultures are still too young. Perhaps none of them are adjusted. In answer to the question, "Why, then, are they not extinct?" we can comfortably answer, "Because they haven't had enough time." Man has been in existence for many tens of thousands of years, and perhaps even hundreds of thousands; this is much longer than the average for most mammals (about twenty thousand years) and even for most birds (about forty thousand years).

Nothing valid can be said about man without considering cultural influences. Our social structure originated in the very dawn of culture, at a time when men like ourselves did not yet exist. We have evidence of culture going back two million years, while definite proof of beings with an anatomy like ours goes back only some tens of thousands of years. The development of the human hand has proceeded parallel with the development of tools: both developments become manifest shortly after the assumption of the erect posture. In fact, the rudiments of technology, if by technology we mean the use of instruments, appear in history much earlier than the first hominids. For example, the female of one species of wasp of the genus *Ammophila* holds a small pebble in her jaws and uses it like a hammer to level off the ground where she will build a depository for her eggs. The woodpecker finch *Camarhychus pallidus,* one of the species found by Darwin in the Galápagos islands, uses a cactus thorn to dig out insects from the bark of trees. The South Sea otter swims about clasping a stone, which is used to crush the shells of the shell-fish which are its diet. In Kenya, the so-called Egyptian vulture takes up a stone with which it may fly a great distance to drop it on ostrich eggs, which it then devours. Goodall found that chimpanzees use a dried plant like a sponge to draw water from places where they cannot drink directly; they also strip twigs of their leaves and use them to gather white ants, of which they are very fond, from cracks where they have hidden. This technique is especially important because apparently it is handed down from parents to young by imitation.

Such extra-biological skills appear essential to the survival of some animals and birds. The hooded monkey living in a natural state depends upon stones to break open certain types of hard-rinded fruits. The ant-eating lion *Myrmeleon formicaleo* relies almost entirely on the use of branches to gather his food. It is common to observe a sea gull snatch up a mollusk from the shore, fly three or four meters into the air, and drop it on a pebbled beach. If it fails to smash open, the bird picks it up in its beak once again and flies a little higher before dropping it, repeating the process until the shell breaks.[1] Many other examples could be provided.

The dexterity of anthropoids is not confined to the search for food. Let us quote two well-attested examples.

A chimpanzee named Jack, in London zoo, seemed to bear ill-will toward persons in conspicuous uniforms. The head of a foreign state was to visit the zoo, and the chimpanzee's cage was cleaned with particular care. When the dignitary and his elaborately uniformed suite passed by, Jack thrust a hand between his legs and threw what he obtained from this source with such good aim that he caused a diplomatic outrage.

A gorilla in the Zoological Gardens of Berlin caught hold of one of the keepers and was doing him serious injury. Toto, a chimpanzee who shared the cage, immediately snatched up the keeper's whip and began to beat the gorilla with such persistence that the keeper was able to escape.

These skills are used in self-defense. Chimpanzees in the natural state have been observed, on a number of occasions, to pick up a stout branch and hold it in the manner of a stave to beat off the attack of a leopard.

Such dexterity is shared in lesser degree by all the primates because they have developed an opposed thumb which permits them to grasp objects skillfully and securely. This and the placing of both eyes in the same plane of sight, permitting a perception of depth, are traits which man shares with them. His own particular trait is his invariable habit of erect movement, which permanently frees his hands, and his capacity for crossing his eyes, a curious faculty of extreme importance for the use and manufacture of objects, since it permits a close examination of objects in focus and without doubling of images. Moreover, man's erect posture is the only one that permits him to support without undue strain the heavy skull needed for a large brain.

With these traits, and a pronounced tendency toward social life, which was characteristic of the first hunters, the human prototypes were endowed with the requirements necessary for the great cultural adventure. An increase in the conventionalization of human behavior, going far beyond that of the nonhuman primates, must have occurred. This implies the development of a standard of conduct involving diversified rules and signal codes in the various cultures and based on an inherited process of elaborate socialization. It also implies an ontogenetic development of a species of superego in personality development. Animals, as Rapoport has pointed out, rarely eat themselves sick. But for human beings, eating can have a symbolic value quite divorced from physiological need. Similarly, animals attack each other because they really are being threatened. But human beings, with a much greater capacity for manipulating symbols, may label whole classes of fellow humans as "enemies" where no real threat from them exists.[2]

What occurs next has no parallel in the entire world of nature. If we consider, following the modern trends among naturalists, that the interplay of a living being with his environment, like all his behavior, is as worthy of description and classification as his morphology or physiology, we have to admit that the *evolution* in the human species of that interplay with the environment and of that behavior belongs to a new order. This order cannot be understood merely by applying the standards of biological evolution. Its essential feature is the preservation and transmission of what has been acquired by experience, using experience in the widest possible sense to cover not only practical knowledge but religious magic, imaginative and emotional experience, and other such qualities of life.

As is well known, Darwin's genius consisted partly in having exposed the errors of the theories of biology elaborated before him, and in particular those of Lamarck, which implied that acquired characteristics are hereditary. The shopworn phrase "function creates the organ," generally held to express the essence of Lamarckism, implies a kind of biological evolutionism. And Lamarck did maintain that a much-used organ will tend to become more highly developed in the offspring than it was originally in their remote ancestors, since each generation of progeny inherits the additional development acquired by its parents.

Darwin proved that Nature does not operate in this fashion. He showed how the changes observed over many generations in animals could only be attributed to elimination of the less adapted variants and accumulation of the traits of the best adapted. In Darwinian biology, the adaptation of an organ to a function was a result reached by a circuitous route involving the gradual elimination of other possible but less efficient solutions, and not by direct organic change toward a desired end. Modern genetics has fully confirmed what Darwin grasped, and although many people still continue to confuse the legal and biological meanings of "inheritance," no scientist now believes that we can "hand down" in a biological sense to our progeny anything that we have acquired after our birth—or to be more precise, our conception—in the same way as it is possible to bequeath property and wealth. The son of a famous pianist has no better chance, biologically speaking, of success as a musician than does any of his cousins. In fact, the cousins have a better chance if their parents encourage them to take music lessons, while the famous pianist wants his son to pursue some other kind of career.

The difference between these two meanings of "heritage" is basic to the separation of heredity from environment. In biology, all heredity is genetic, that is, it comes through the genes, with a hereditary structure insofar as it is already established at the moment of birth. Biologists thus differentiate the physical constitution transmitted by genes, called the *genotype,* from the personal characteristics of the individual, called the *phenotype.* The phenotype, remaining within the framework bounded by the genotype, leaves a margin of mobility for the development of acquired traits, which are genetically non-transferable. Thus a black-haired woman may spend her life dyeing her hair, but this will not affect her genotype, which will transmit to her descendants a characteristic for black hair. On the other hand, the widely discussed and dramatic mutations triggered by the drug thalidomide may directly change the genotype without affecting the phenotype in the slightest; the mothers of the mutant babies showed no evidence of change, and it was only in their offspring that the new mutations developed. Biological evolution, contrary to the almost magical infallibility sometimes attributed to it, does not always work in favor of survival. For instance, when a human being is afflicted by kidney stones—certainly a threat to his survival—the attempt to pass them from the kidney to the bladder is often blocked by acute spasms in the ureters. This can easily be fatal if not handled by modern medical procedures. If evolution is all that it is said to be, why hasn't this particular reaction been eliminated?

With respect to environment, it is obvious that culture is also subject to evolution, and more noticeably so than nature. Comparison of the appearance of the human shape of the sixteenth century with our unchanged appearance today, juxtaposed with the enormous gulf between the fashions, society, art and science of that period and those of our own, will give an idea of the relative speed of change. And since culture *is* subject to evolution, it is only logical to compare it with biological evolution. Is there, then, a selective cultural mechanism at work, like the one that effects the transformation of species? If such a mechanism does exist, it operates in a manner directly opposite to that of its biological counterpart, for in cultural evolution it is the acquired characteristics that are passed on. Of course, these two types of evolution are not wholly independent of each other. It is undeniable that culture develops when a certain point in biological evolution is reached, nor is biological evolution halted by it, but rather continues to build up the substratum for further evolution. As biological beings, our evolution has not concluded. The biological changes we may still undergo might change the biological substrata on which our culture is based and bring about radical cultural transformations. But, in view of the different rhythms of these two kinds of evolution, it is more likely that it will be culture that will exert a decisive influence on our living conditions, so changing them that we will either have to adapt biologically in a selective manner or come into open conflict with our environment.

This opposition between two evolutions, or between two heritages, as it were, is what makes Leroi-Gourhan say that culture is the exteriorization of memory.[3] Using the word "memory" in its broadest sense, it can be said that biological memory is in the genes. If we disregard behavior that, in superior animals, might perhaps be considered to display a rudimentary form of culture, we can say that an animal possesses all of his behavior patterns at birth. That is what we mean by saying that animal behavior is instinctive. The mice of China or of Mexico, of the fifteenth century or of the twentieth, will always react according to their patterns. But a human being will behave in a manner according to the culture in which he has been raised. If we observe the life of social insects—bees, for example—we find a complex behavior and a very elaborate organization, in many ways comparable to ours. But there is a radical difference that prevents us from speaking of the "culture" of the bees: at birth a bee is already equipped with all of its norms of conduct and, even if raised in isolation, its behavior patterns will be identical because they do not have to be learned. A child, on the other hand, is born with only a part of his behavior patterns: the biological part that we share with all animals. In order to become fully human he needs an education, beginning with the learning of the language, which actually constitutes a second gestation; that is why some have called education "the social uterus." A fine illustration of this is the tale of the Emperor Akbar of India who, in the sixteenth century, wanted to prove that, with no interference from other "corrupted" languages men would naturally speak the language of God. He ordered that a group of children be educated by deaf-mute women, without ever being taught a spoken language. The result was that the children learned to communicate by means of sign language, as used by the women who took care of them.

Every human being learns that one of the best ways of evaluating information that one possesses about one's environment, about oneself, about the consequences of one's acts, about other people and about the relative possibilities of various future events, is to trust the information provided by others. The major part of human comprehension of the environment, physical as well as social, is not obtained by means of a person's direct experiences, but by the information transmitted to him by other members of the group.

Leroi-Gourhan concludes that, if a parallel is to be established between biological and cultural evolution, at any rate, one should not compare the cultural history of humanity with the evolutionary history of a species. On the historical level, the nearest equivalent to a biological species is a group of the same origin and the same cultural tradition. Ethnologists call these "ethnic groups"; in them, tradition functions as an *exteriorized memory,* in which the behavior patterns that the group will inherit are inscribed. Thanks to this exteriorization, the acquired experience is allowed to pass into the group's collective memory, and is thereby transmitted from one generation to another. But from the evolutionary point of view, each ethnic group or unit can change in a different and independent way, just as different biological species evolve in independent directions. However, the parallel between biological and cultural evolution is no longer applicable when one is dealing with cultural "cross-breeding," since cross-breeding between two distinct biological species is, as a rule, impossible (though in some species it may be induced under laboratory conditions). Moreover, man can adapt to so many different ecological niches by means of his culture that Erikson, for instance, has referred to cultures as "pseudospecies."[4] We shall subsequently develop this concept. It helps to explain how a human being can perceive his enemy, a member of the same species against whom he wages war, much as other animals see the members of different species with which they deal in predatory fashion. Here we are only interested in pointing out that we have as yet neither a behavioral nor a cultural taxonomy to which we can refer with exactitude. Now that we know there is no dichotomy between behavior and function, or between instinct and learning, we find ourselves in what might be described as a pre-Linnean era in the systematic study of behavior. If we are to draw closer to a knowledge of man's true evolution, we shall have to construct a behavioral taxonomy that can be integrated with evolutionary taxonomy.

The stage that we have reached in this inquiry can now be summarized as follows. Since man is characterized by unity of biological species coupled with great cultural diversity, we can never know precisely with what, in the whole of nature, to compare his behavior. If we try to compare the aggressive behavior of human beings with that of animals that live in groups, the specifically human cultural elements make the dissimilarities more striking than the similarities. For example: animals that fight with those of their own species to obtain dominance, territory, or females, always meet in "fair fight"; there are never any fights of many against one. "Clearly," states Rapoport, "the attempts to explain man's inhumanity to man, basing the explanations on his carnivorous origins, do not in any way justify cannibalism."[5] The death of an enemy among animals is a rare accident. Assassination is unthinkable in nature, while human aggressiveness cannot be imagined without some connection, whether it be direct or indirect, with killing.

If, on the other hand, we wish to compare war among ethnic groups, nations, or peoples with the predatory behavior of animal species, we find, on closer examination, that the similarity between these two areas of behavior is an imaginary one, created by our own habits and prejudices. To speak of a "struggle" for existence is a distorted manner of describing things. Natural selection operates by means of homeostatic equilibrium and by automatic birth control, not by killing. Given the opportunity, the other animal species always live in the maximum harmony possible—something that cannot be said about peoples and nations.

As for *individual* aggression among human beings, we cannot see it merely as an instinct, because man *is* his culture. Again, in aggression between cultural groups, we cannot perceive merely a competition among "species," because all human cultures are works of the same species. When people speak of the biological necessity of war we can never tell if they are comparing it with natural selection, with hunting, with hierarchical dominance, or with the so-called survival of the fittest. Hunting itself is in many aspects the opposite of war: in nature, a homeostatic equilibrium tends to exist between hunter and hunted, since nothing is more contrary to biological interest than the extinction of the prey as a species. But in the history of mankind there are many examples of the total disappearance of a people.

In an experiment, dogs and rabbits were left at liberty on a small island. It was found that a balance was maintained in their numbers without the extermination of either group. The birth rate in the dogs diminished when rabbits became scarce, and increased when the rabbits, hunted by the dogs, again began to multiply. Indeed, this phenomenon, which has been observed in experiments with many animals and insects, can be described with mathematical exactness. Brown concludes that the dog population adjusted its size to the availability of resources with the sensitivity of a thermostat controlling the temperature of a room.[6] No thermostat, however, appears to have controlled the conduct of the civilized men who destroyed the Inca and the Mesopotamian cultures.

NOTES

1. K.P. Oakley, "Skill as a Human Possession," in G. Singer, L.J. Homyard, and A.R. Hall (eds.), *History of Technology* (Oxford, 1954).

2. Anatol Rapoport, review of Carthy and Ebling (eds.), *The Natural History of Aggression,* in *Scientific American,* 213, 115–6, 1965.

3. André Leroi-Gourhan, *Le geste et la parole* (Paris, 1965).

4. E.H. Erikson, "Ontogeny of Ritualization," *Philosophical Transactions of the Royal Society of London,* Series B, 1966.

5. Rapoport, op. cit.

6. Roger Brown, *Social Psychology* (New York, 1965).

6

RACISM
1. The Fallacy of Biological Racism

The least defensible and also the most deeply rooted prejudice hampering peaceful relations among men is probably the racial one. It can be traced back to the earliest times of which historical records have survived. The Pharaoh Sesostris (1887–1849 B.C.) put a stone marker on the southern boundary of Egypt that prohibited the entrance of all Negroes to the country. Aristotle (384–322 B.C.), basing his opinion on the supposed influences of climate, concluded that the Nordic peoples (precisely those who, at the present day, might be so proud of their "Aryan blood") were destined by nature to slavery. Cicero (106–43 B.C.), although he had maintained that "men differ in their knowledge, not in their aptitude for knowledge," lets himself be dominated all the same by this prejudice when he affirms, for instance, that the Celts are "stupid and incapable of being taught." These attitudes were carried by Europeans to the New World. In 1550 Ginés de Sepúlveda commented on the "natural inferiority and perversity of the American Indians," asserting that they were not "rational beings" and that the Indians were "as different from the Spaniards as . . . . apes are from men." Opposing this position there were a few isolated figures like Fray Bartolomé de las Casas, who maintained that all the peoples of the earth consisted of the same kind of men, and fought for the abolition of slavery for Indians as well as for Negroes, "because reason is with them as it is with the Indians."

During the Enlightenment, in spite of the defense of man's equality by Voltaire, Rousseau, Buffon, and others, an outstanding thinker like Hume could still maintain that Negroes were inferior to whites. In Europe, this prejudice lived on in spite of the Christian tradition, clearly anti-racist, as expressed by St. Paul in his famous speech at Athens: ". . . and hath made of one blood all nations of men for to dwell on all the face of the earth" (Acts 17:26). It was also St. Paul who wrote: "There is neither Jew nor Greek, there is neither bond nor free, there is neither male nor female: for ye are all one in Christ Jesus" (Gal. 3:28). Despite this, a certain Reverend Thomas Thompson published in 1772 a pamphlet entitled *How the trade in negro slaves on the African coast respects the principles of humanity and the laws of revealed religion.* In 1852 the Reverend Josiah Priest published a similar attempt at religious justification called

A Biblical Reference of Slavery. Many other such works could be cited. As late as 1900, one C. Carrol brought out a book with the title *The Negro a Beast or Anti-image of God*, in which he affirmed that all scientific evidence proved that the constitution of Negroes was completely apelike. In the twentieth century, however, Christian doctrine has progressed somewhat: Pius XI condemned racism, and an encyclical of Pius XII, in 1938, called it apostasy.

SO-CALLED SCIENTIFIC RACISM

During the years 1853–1855, not long before the appearance of *The Origin of Species*, the French diplomat Joseph Arthur de Gobineau published his *Essay on the Inequality of Human Races*, and so introduced the doctrine that "pure," or unmixed races were naturally superior to mixed ones. In Europe, the "master race" was supposed to be that of the Aryans—a theory the consequences of which in our times are known to all. The theory was immediately adopted and propagated by Richard Wagner, and subsequently by H. S. Chamberlain, his English son-in-law.

To grasp the depth of racial prejudice in the nineteenth century it is enough to know that no less a man than Abraham Lincoln once said: "There is a physical difference between the white and black races which I believe will always forbid that the two peoples should live together in social and political equality."[1] But racism—at least white racism—took a new turn after the appearance of Darwinism. "The whites" accepted Darwin with enthusiasm; to them, he confirmed their policy of expansion and aggression at the expense of "inferior" peoples.

In the twentieth century, with its history of class conflict, it has become clear that the ideas of natural selection and natural superiority, more or less based on Darwin's thesis, can even be used within an ethnic group. Thus Erich Suchsland upholds the thesis that individuals who have not been successful in life necessarily belong to the "inferior" racial elements of the population, while the rich belong to a "superior race." Juan Comas comments ironically upon this theory that, if it is true, systematic bombing of the poorer quarters in every city would result in improvement of the race through selection.[2] A line of reasoning similar to Suchsland's is followed by Alexis Carrel, the renowned author of *Man the Unknown*, who asserts that proletarians and the unemployed are "inferior" peoples because of their natural heritage. Since they have poor constitutions, he says, they do not have the strength to struggle —indeed, they have fallen so low that further struggles have become useless.

It is hardly worth dwelling on Hitler's racism; the terrible memories he left still haunt the world. It would perhaps be better to quote some rather droll facts about the conclusions drawn by racist theorists, if we can possibly forget for a moment the tragic consequences of these ideas when put into practice by Nazi fanatics. Waltmann affirmed that Jesus had Aryan blood, or in any case was not the son of a Jew like Joseph, since Jesus had no human father. The same author deformed the names of many of mankind's geniuses (presumably he also deformed their physical traits somewhat) in order to demonstrate that they were really Teutons: for Giotto, Jothe; for Dante Alighieri, Aigler; for Da Vinci, Wincke; for Tasso, Dasse; for Michelangelo Buonarotti, Bohurodt; for Velázquez, Valchise; for Murillo, Moerl; for Diderot, Tiestroh; and others. Otto Ammon asserted that dolichocephalous men (like the Aryans) are "socially superior" to brachycephalous men (like the so-called Alpine type), and that for this reason the dolichocephalous were concentrated in greater proportion in the cities than in the country and belonged to the privileged classes and not to the working classes. There may have been some truth in the proposition that the German population was distributed in this way, though not for the reasons given by Ammon. Indeed, had he followed his own theories consistently, he would have been forced to conclude that the Aryan race was naturally destined to be ruled by Negroes who are, in fact, the human race's most dolichocephalous men! If he ever concluded anything of the sort, he certainly kept quiet about it. A like dilemma was faced by Kaiser Wilhelm II, who commissioned anthropometric studies of the Germans to demonstrate the "purity and superiority" of the Aryan race. The studies were carried out but were never published because there turned out to be entire areas without a single "Aryan" specimen. Another German researcher conceived the plan of dividing mankind into three castes: the pure-blooded Germans, who would enjoy all the political and social privileges; those with "more or less German" blood, who would enjoy limited privileges; and those who were not German, who would be deprived of every political right and sterilized to save civilization. It is hard to imagine anybody taking this fanatical absurdity any further. But there was someone who did: F. K. Gunther, theoretician of Hitler's racism, who seriously proposed to draw a neat dividing line between the "Nordic" man and the entire animal kingdom, to which naturally the rest of "non-Nordic" mankind would belong. More vaudevillian (as usual) was Mussolini's claim that there existed a pure Italian race of the "Aryan-Nordic" type. But the nonsense did not stop there. Impelled by political necessity, Aryanist theoreticians went as far as to say that the Japanese were Teutons! In this account, the Japanese became descendants of the white Ainus who had become mixed with the yellow races. This did not prevent them, as the Nazi theoretician Rosenberg wrote, from "possessing all the moral and intellectual qualities of an Aryan or even Nordic group. . . . the Japanese leaders offer the same biological guarantees as the German leaders."

But the absurdity of the Nazi racist thesis hardly needs further demonstration. The Nazis themselves became entangled in so many contradictions that finally they were forced to say that race was a mystical and intuitive concept that transcended mere scientific proof. Since it was clearly absurd, from any reasonable point of view, to have a Teutonic archetype as fair as Hitler, as tall as Goebbels, and as slim as Goering, the Nazis found a way out by affirming that "a Nordic soul can inhabit a non-Nordic body," and that "politics must come before science, confirmed by the fundamental intuitive truth of blood differences among all peoples and entailing, as a logical consequence, the principle of government by the fittest."

THE CONCEPT OF RACE

Racism is not always as evident nor as extremist as in its Nazi form. But it is often extremely difficult to argue with racists who think they have logical and objective proof of their theories, but are really only rationalizing their prejudices. In our age, this type of rationalization is frequently based on an imperfect grasp of Darwinism. The false conclusions carelessly drawn from the natural selection thesis seem to fall under two main heads: (1) the supposedly harmful character of hybridization, or race mixture; (2) the alleged natural superiority of some races in regard to others.

The first group of prejudices is based on the false premise that there are pure races. To begin with, the very concept of race is scientifically rather vague. What *is* clear, biologically speaking, is that all living men belong to the same species, and that within this species there are individual and group variations. Some of the group variations serve as criteria to determine the classification of various groups into what we call races.

Biologists, however, do not yet agree as to which group variations should serve as criteria. Sometimes the following are considered: blood reactions, average height, relative proportions of parts of the body, color of skin, texture and color of hair, width of nose. Sometimes only a few of these traits are considered, sometimes others are included. Selection of the features to be compared is necessarily arbitrary. The classification principle in itself is also arbitrary: the number of races and sub-races varies from one author to another. Furthermore, the concept cannot be static, because the races are constantly changing because of regrouping, selection, and adaptation within the group as well as through admixtures of external origin. Thus, a "race" is a changing biological phenomenon that can be understood only within an evolving context, with reference to environmental and genetic parameters that are constantly shifting.

But no matter what system of classification we use or how we arrive at it, it would be impossible, even by going very far into the past, to find a pure race. Even at the dawn of mankind, men belonging to very different groups used to mix. From then on there is interbreeding and crossbreeding without limit. Pure races, in the sense of genetically homogeneous societies, do not exist in the human species.[3] If we take a single feature as the criterion of race membership, then it may be found that in certain groups statistically significant proportions of individuals possess it. But the moment we consider several features together, the proportion of individuals in any group who possess them turns out to be very much lower. For example, it is a common belief among Mexicans that Englishmen have light eyes. Actually, only one out of five Englishmen has this feature.[4] Moreover, the genetic composition of the British population is extremely mixed: citing only the largest contributors we find elements of Cro-Magnon, Nordic, Mediterranean, and Alpine origin, together with more recent admixtures from Saxon, Norwegian, Danish, and Norman groups. When the English colonized North America the result was an even greater mixture. American Negroes are no "purer," racially speaking, than American whites: their ancestry is Congolese Bantu, western European, Siberian, and Mediterranean, among others. As regards the Jews, they were already a rather mixed group during Biblical times, and the Diaspora produced so much hybridization that the majority of Jews have racial traits more like those of the people of the countries where they live than like those of Jews in other countries.[5] Thus, in spite of their assertions as to the intuitive recognition of racial superiority, the Nazis were forced to make the Jews wear a Star of David so that they could distinguish them from the Aryans, who were supposed to belong to another species.

But even if we choose to disregard the ambiguity of the race concept and the universality of human hybridization, and even if we wish to say that, in some mystical and intuitive way, we can decide which are the "real" races and in what their purity consists, we still have to prove that crossbreeding between these supposedly pure races is harmful. The thesis of its harmfulness was sustained by Y. A. Mjonn; he has many followers in the United States, among them S. K. Humphrey, M. Grant, and L. Stoddard. Besides the genetic, typological, and statistical inaccuracy of these studies, their data is interpreted on the basis of a crude error which amounts to confusing the consequences with the causes. In all those countries where so-called half-breeds are discriminated against, it is obvious that the worst social traits are found among them with disproportionate frequency. But this is because the most dismal material and cultural conditions are imposed upon them. Furthermore, discrimination results in a greater proportion of crossbreeding among the socially depressed classes. Lundborg[6] and Schreider[7] have amply proved this fact.

From the point of view of the science of genetics, all these ideas are merely aberrations. Endogamy (that is, breeding between members of the same social group) is not of itself any likelier to improve animal "races" than its opposite, exogamy. Crossing, or crossbreeding does have the immediate effect of preventing the external manifestation of the recessive traits peculiar to one or other of the crossed races. Endogamous aristocratic families, as we have seen, do tend to exhibit such traits; interbreeding between members of the same family origin reinforces both the "best" and the "worst" traits of the group. In the long run, endogamy is the more likely to be harmful. It is true that through endogamy there is an accumulation of the traits that have so far insured the group's survival. But if the environment changes, these traits will lose value, and the accumulation of recessive traits, or taints, which also results from endogamy, dooms the group to eventual extinction. Concerning crossbreeding, however, Juan Comas has the following conclusions:

(1) Crossbreeding has existed since the dawn of mankind.
(2) Crossbreeding permits numerous new combinations of genetic factors, which produce a salutory flexibility in the hereditary qualities of the new population.
(3) Highly civilized regions are inhabited, for the most part, by groups of very mixed genetic composition.[8]

SKIN COLOR.

From the point of view of purely physical or physiological aptitudes we discover a similar situation: the differences between races compensate for the environmental disadvantages peculiar to each race. Thus white people generally bear dry heat better than black Africans, who are more resistant to humid heat. The resistance of Lapps to the cold is well known; less well known is the fact that Australian aborigines casually sleep in the open air at temperatures close to zero, although their extremities are generally colder than those of Europeans, who cannot sleep safely under such conditions.

But the most striking physical difference between races, and the one in which racism has the greatest emotional investment, is that of skin color. Modern biology has proved that this is no more immutable than other superficial physical differences. Lerner has shown that the color of frogs' skins changes radically upon the injection of certain hormones.[9] A frog submerged in water containing melatonin becomes almost black. The injected hormone stimulates the melanocites, which are dermal cells producing melanine in varying quantities. In human beings, it has been found that both blue and brown eyes contain the same number of melanocites, but that those of brown eyes produce more melanine. Moreover, the hormone that stimulates melanocites in frogs has similar effects on human beings. Men injected with appreciable amounts of these hormones began to turn black after twenty-four hours. Daily doses caused further darkening up to the point when they were suspended. The skin recovered its original color three to five weeks after the last injection. In other experiments, black-haired rats turned white when subjected to a diet of phenil-tio-urea. Such results have led Coon to believe that it will be possible to change our skin coloring at will within the near future.[10]

CULTURE INDEPENDENT OF RACE.

There is a very marked general tendency to associate similar racial features with similar cultures and, of course, to ascribe cultural variation to racial differences. The following data illustrate the folly of such generalizations.

Contrasting Racial Types: Same Cultural Features

(1) Masked dancers who personify supernatural beings and whose identity is kept secret from women and children:

    a. Pueblo Indian Kachinas (Hopi, Zuñi)

    b. Melanesia in general (but especially New Britain).

(2) Taboo on speaking with or being in the presence of (or even in the same house as) the mother-in-law:

    a. Chiricahua Apaches.

    b. Murngin from Arnhem (northern Australia).

(3) Beating instrument used as a sign of supreme power:

    a. Hammer of Thor, supreme god of the Scandinavian Pantheon.

    b. Hatchet of Shango, supreme god of the Dahomeyans.

    c. Polynesian hatchet, called tiki, insignia of the chiefs.

(4) Burial in urns:

    a. Guaraní of Paraguay (without cremation).

    b. Culture of urn burial grounds (with cremation, A.D. 800-1200) in southern Germany (probably a product of the Celtic groups).

(5) Cultivation basically dependent upon the corn, squash, and bean complex:

    a. Middle America.

    b. Angola and the southern Congo.

(6) Sacrifice of hens (almost always black) for healing purposes, or for appeasing supernatural beings in various circumstances (for example when constructing a house):

    a. Dahomey.

    b. Tzeltales, Tzotziles, the Otomies of San Pablito and of the Sierra of Puebla.

Same Racial Type:
Contrasting Cultural Features

(1) *a.* In the United States, corn is consumed in various forms such as corn flakes and sweet corn. In some European countries, for example in Italy, it is used for polenta.

    b. In Belgium, the people preferred to starve at the end of the Second World War rather than eat corn, which they considered "food for pigs." (Corn is cultivated in Belgium, although not on a large scale, as feed for hogs.)

(2) *a.* In nearly all of Europe, as in a good portion of America, in part of Africa, and even in the western part of India, wheat is the basic nutritional cereal.

    b. In the state of Assam, in eastern India, serious

disturbances broke out in 1966 due to a scarcity of rice. According to newspaper reports, the people were saying, "If they can't give us rice, let them shoot us." They refused to consume the wheat sent by other countries and by the wheat-producing zone in India.

(3) *a.* Blacksmiths are considered outcasts by the Masai tribe of east Africa; they must camp separately, are subject to all types of insults, and are never permitted to marry a pure Masai woman.

    b. Among the Bambera or the Fon of the Dahomey, blacksmiths are held in very high esteem and enjoy special privileges.

(4) *a.* Among the Ashanti (in Ghana), estate inheritance is through the mother's side of the family.

    b. Among the rest of the groups of west Africa, inheritance is through the father's side.

(5) *a.* The diet of the tribes of the northeast coast of North America (such as Nutka and Tlingit) is based on fish.

    b. Among the tribes of the southwestern United States (the Hopi, for example), there is still a taboo against eating fish.

(6) *a.* Among the peoples of Central Asia (the Kirghiz and Cossacks, for example) milk and its derivatives are popular and are consumed in large quantities.

    b. In eastern central China there is a general absence of milking and of the use of milk or any milk products.

POVERTY AND BIOLOGY.

Recent studies have shown that most cases of arrested brain development in the first four years of life are due to protein or calorie deficiencies, not genes. Children with exceptionally severe deficiencies of this kind, if they do not die, are incapacitated for life. This is because 95 percent of brain growth occurs by the end of the fourth year. And undernourished mothers produce children with life-long disabilities attributable to malnutrition.

A study of fifty children from the slums of Cape Town is representative of hundreds undertaken in the last decade.[11] Half of the children had been grossly undernourished during their earliest years, mainly through parental neglect. The others lived in poverty, but had been somewhat better fed. All were studied over an eleven-year period. On intelligence tests, sixty percent of the undernourished children scored below the level of even the lowest-scoring better fed children, and only one exceeded the latters' mean score. All the children were somewhat handicapped in verbal ability, but the severely undernourished were also handicapped in mathematical ability, visual perception, and eye-hand coordination. They also had smaller heads, on the average, which means—according to the following test—that they had smaller brains. In a normal baby, a bright light held against the head produces a narrow translucent zone through the skull cap. In a child with advanced malnutrition, this translucent zone is much larger, reaching practically the whole skull. Apparently some of the space that should be filled with brains fills up with spinal fluid instead. Thus the damage done by malnutrition at this stage can never be repaired.

The worldwide effect of malnutrition on human development cannot be accurately measured at the present time. But it is clearly very great. Nearly two-thirds of the world's population—about 2.1 billion people—live in countries where the annual per capita income is below $300, and over ninety percent of these in countries where it is below $200. Of course, the poverty line is drawn in different places in countries with different standards of living; in the USA, for instance, it works out at $750 per capita in an average family of four. It is impossible to tell without further information whether the American poor are more undernourished than those of Portuguese Angola, where the per capita income is $56. Nevertheless, it is certain that many and perhaps most human populations suffer from brain impairment connected with malnutrition because they also suffer from poverty. It is this cruel fact that provides unscrupulous pseudoscientific observers with "proof" that this or that biological group is inherently inferior. It is true, for instance, that the infants of poor mothers are some fifteen percent smaller on the average than those of mothers who are better off.[12] But what matters here is food, not genes.

NOTES

1. Speech delivered at Charleston, December 18, 1858.

2. Juan Comas, "Les mythes raciaux," in *Le racisme devant la science* (Paris, UNESCO, 1960), pp. 13-58.

3. Santiago Genovés (ed.), "Race and Racism: the Third Conference of UNESCO," *Yearbook of Physical Anthropology,* 13, 270-280, 1965.

4. Comas, op. cit.

5. Ibid.

6. Herman Lundborg, "Hybrid Types of the Human Race," *Journal of Heredity,* 12, 274-80, 1921.

7. Eugene Schreider, *La biologie humaine* (Paris, 1964).

8. Comas, op. cit.

9. A.B. Lerner, "Skin Pigmentation," *Scientific American,* 205, 98-112, 1961.

10. Carleton Coon, *The Origin of Races* (New York, 1962).

11. For this and other such studies see David C. Glass (ed.), *Biology and Behavior* (New York, 1968).

12. R.L. Naeye and others, "Urban Poverty: Effects on Prenatal Nutrition," *Science,* 166, p. 1026, 1969.

7

RACISM
2. Prejudices Centered on Race

Most Europeans and whites of European ancestry take the superiority of their culture for granted. It is hard to see why they should be so complacent. Other cultures have produced an abundance of solutions that appear far more adequate or intelligent than those applied by Western culture to the same problems. For example, according to Gough the Nayer tribe of southern India has solved the problem of endogamy and exogamy in the following ingenious fashion. Before reaching puberty, the girls are wed, en masse, to men of another group. They probably never go to live with their husbands nor do they ever see them again, in spite of the fact that a wife performs mourning ceremonies when her "husband" dies. The girls take lovers appropriate to their social standing and the children that result from these unions stay with their mothers. The Nayers trace the line of descent through the mother; the heads of families are brothers of the married women who do not cohabit with them, but take lovers from among women who are not related to them in any way.[1]

Among the Kulus and other tribes of the Himalayan Mountains, polyandry frequently occurs and is generally fraternal, that is, several brothers have one wife in common. When all of the brothers are present in the house, the wife usually confers her favors upon each one of them in turn. The house usually has two rooms, one for the wife and the other for the husbands. When one brother enters the room of the wife, he leaves his shoes or his hat at the door, the equivalent of putting up a "do not disturb" sign. Similarly, when there are quarrels between the women of the Jat tribe of the Punjab, one of them usually says to the other: "You are so neglectful of your duties that you don't even take the brothers of your husband into your arms!"[2]

Marco Polo ridiculed the Chinese for having wasted their discovery of gunpowder on fireworks. But the Chinese could equally well have doubted the intelligence of people who employed explosives for the destruction of human life.

All observers who have studied the way of life of the Aleuts speak of their honesty, their gentleness, their love for their wives and children, their pacific character. Physical punishment of children does not exist among them; the stories they tell to little children often show that they value knowledge above all things. Nevertheless, Shade relates that a little girl told him that she did not intend to teach her children the Aleut tongue "because the white men make fun of the people that speak it." Can we sincerely believe that these white men are so superior?

It is hard to obtain reliable experimental data about human cultures; only dictators move whole peoples from one environment to another without consulting them. But in the plant world, at least, it seems clear that no species or variety can claim superiority in any absolute sense. In experiments undertaken by Turresson,[3] and by Clausen[4] and his associates, cuttings were taken from growing plants found in different regions. Each was divided into three or more cuttings (leaving aside mutations, the cuttings from any one plant are of similar genotypes) and these were replanted in different geographical environments: one at sea level, another in a temperate climate, and the third in an alpine or mountainous zone. The plants originating at sea level proved completely incapable of surviving in the alpine zone, where the warm season was too short to allow them to produce flowers and germinate. The alpine plants showed improved growth in the intermediate zone and at sea level over the plants native to those regions. The conclusion, then, is that the observed differences between plants native to different altitudes are partly genetic and partly a consequence of the environment.

More often than not, racial prejudice does not bother to justify itself by warning of the supposed evils of crossbreeding, discussed in the previous chapter. It simply and openly declares certain races superior to others. In our epoch it is most common to affirm the superiority of the white race, while the black race is an habitual object of contempt. However, in more general terms, all "colored" races, to a greater or lesser degree, are seen as inferior by white people. As recently as 1919, the humanitarian delegates who attended the Paris Conference during which the League of Nations was created, refused to accept a declaration proposed by the Japanese delegation which proclaimed the equality of all races.

The most immediate and common expression of this prejudice refers to intelligence. The first point to make in this context is that all experimental testing of intelligence is radically ambiguous, confused, and finally tautological. Given that intelligence, like any other psychological characteristic, can only be defined by means of quantifiable tests, and that these tests cannot, in their turn, be based upon a necessarily unknown predetermined definition, one deduces that the only thing a psychological test can reveal is the capacity to solve precisely the test itself and no more, a capacity which can only arbitrarily be identified with intelligence. Indeed, another research worker may well suppose that the capacity to solve the test depends not upon intelligence but stupidity. This was the experience of an investigator sent to administer such a test among the poor white children of Kentucky. He set them Binet's well known problem: "If you went to the store. and bought six cents' worth of candies, and gave the store-

114

keeper ten cents, how much change would you get?"
One boy replied: "I've never had ten cents and if I had
I wouldn't spend them on candies. Anyway, ma makes
the candies." The examiner tried again and set the
problem anew: "If you took ten of your father's cows
out to graze and six got lost, how many would you take
back home?" The child answered: "We don't have ten
cows, but if we had and I lost six of them, I would not
dare go home." The examiner made a last try: "If there
were ten children in school and six of them got the
mumps, how many would be left in school?" This time
the answer came more quickly: "Not one, because the
others would stay away for fear of catching it."[5] Fortu-
nately, in this case the investigator was an imaginative
man and did not infer that the child was stupid, but that
the tests were.

The same kinds of tests have been used to justify
racial prejudice. But Brigham and Goodenough, who
right after the First World War asserted that there are
racial differences in intelligence, later recanted precisely because they found that to try to measure innate
intelligence is perfectly absurd. The search for a test
that will be free of cultural influence, whether an intelligence test or any other test that tries to measure fixed
traits, is an illusion; the naive supposition that freedom
from verbal requisites makes a test equally adequate for
all groups can no longer be accepted. The reason for
this is that intelligence itself is largely a product of
culture.

But we need not go so deeply into the discussion of

the scientific proof of these tests. Even if we admit that they do partially measure intelligence, and that the test scores, graded from "higher" to "lower," do make some sense, it is still true that the only result obtained from all this is precisely that there are no observable differences of superiority or inferiority between races. The observable differences that *do* exist may all be due to certain social, cultural, and accidental factors that have nothing to do with innate qualities. In the first place, all the authorities are agreed that in the psychological field, as well as in the field of physical characteristics, the range of the differences between *individuals* of the same racial group, whether that group is supposedly "pure" or admittedly mixed, is always at least equal and is generally greater than the range of the differences between the *average* measurements for that group and the corresponding averages for other groups. In other words, even if we could establish in a relatively reasonable way that the average intelligence quotient of white people is superior to that of Negroes, this could very well mean that, for example, all whites are at the same mediocre level, while the few geniuses are all Negroes.

However, it is clear that not even this can be established on a reasonable basis. The best-known demonstration of this was provided by the alpha and beta tests that the American army conducted during the First World War. The results showed that many northern Negroes obtained scores higher than those of many southern whites. Since the "races" are the same in both north and south, these differences clearly stem from divergences in cultural and living standards. Montagu proved the evident correlation between these scores and the state educational investment *per capita:* when it was higher than the average, the Negroes invariably obtained higher averages than whites in states where the per capita investment was less.[6] In the same way, certain tests conducted among North American Indians showed an average inferior to that of white children. But when these Indian children were adopted and brought up by white families, their averages were as high as those of white children and higher than those of their brothers who had remained in their parents' families. An even more striking result was obtained among a group of Indian children of the Osage tribe in Oklahoma. These children actually scored higher on language tests than their white counterparts. It may not be a coincidence that the Osage own a number of oil wells.

If the example of the alpha and beta tests is the most often quoted proof that racial superiority is a myth, the opposing evidence least quoted by white racists is probably a series of studies conducted in 1935 by a Japanese professor, Kanichi Tanaka. With official sponsorship, and as many scientific guarantees as the Europeans might have had under the same circumstances, Tanaka arrived at the conclusion that a race superior in intelligence and temperament did exist. One can immediately guess that he was referring to the Japanese race. Naturally, in view of the political situation at that time, the one which followed was the German. Then came—in the following order—the English, the Portuguese, the French, the Hawaiian, the Italian, the Spanish, and the Philippine. The results on the Americans were not published by Tanaka, but he did not keep secret the fact that they were *not* superior to the Japanese. The conclusion of his study was that the Japanese must jealously guard their racial purity, especially when it came to mixing with the Chinese.

One may see, then, how far the abuse of psychological tests can go. It has been repeatedly proved that in the first two years in a child's life, when the differences in actual experience are minimal, there is no significant racial difference as regards intelligence. It is impossible to find out by tests of this type what is due to environment and what to innate qualities; this explains the discrepancy in the results. Intelligence quotient tests have been conducted among American, Chinese, and Hindu students, noting different aspects of this thing called "intelligence." In those aspects of a more innate nature, such as association and retention, the Orientals were superior; in the cultural aspects, the Americans were superior. But, aside from the ambiguity of the term "culture" in this context, what can an American investigator call "culture" if it is not Western culture, and how can we distinguish this "culture" from plain "information," where, for instance, the Hindus tested were better informed than the Americans? During another such test conducted in England in 1938, children of mixed English and Chinese ancestry scored higher than "purebred" English children. In 1932, Binet and Pinther obtained similar results in tests taken among Chinese and American children. Goodenough also found Chinese children superior, but only in certain aspects, such as graphic representation.[7]

Nevertheless, the prejudice persists that some races are at least physically superior and inferior to others. Many whites, for example, think that black-skinned people represent a less advanced evolutionary state than their own. In fact, nothing could be more false. In the first place, the evidence on which such a generalization could be based does not exist; even in the southern United States, as the authors of a recent study point out, it has never been collected.[8] In the second place, if it were collected, as the same authors contend, it is extremely likely that the significant inequalities between so-called racial groups could be removed by purely social measures— better food distribution, for example. The prejudiced eye unfailingly mistakes social effects for biological constants. But to do so is a truly simple-minded version of evolutionism, based on the belief that all the "races" form a natural hierarchy, from the least to the most evolved. In actual fact, every biological group exhibits certain characteristics that are more highly evolved and others that are less highly evolved. Upon comparing the lips of a primate, a white man, and a Negro, it is evident that the white man's lips represent an intermediate state between the primates' and the Negroes'. We should come to the same conclusion if we observed the hair of a gorilla, a white man, and a Negro. The Aryan supremacists used to argue that the more dolichocephalous the shape of the cranium, the more superior it was from a biological standpoint. By this criterion, the Aryans themselves would stand halfway between the Alpine peoples and the Negroes. However, as regards the brain, the form and weight of which can indeed be measured with precision, all human races show precisely the same characteristics: the brain of an Australian aborigine is, on the average, of the same specific weight and is marked by the same convolutions as that of the average student of Cambridge University. The truth is that once brains are out of their respective craniums not even the most expert phrenologist could distinguish them by racial origin. On the other hand, it is completely false to suppose that what we commonly call intelligence bears any relation, among individuals, to the weight or shape of the brain. The weights of the brains of illustrious persons, for instance, vary greatly.

The falsity of racist theories has been firmly denounced in a declaration signed by twenty-two distinguished experts in genetics and anthropology from every part of the world who were called together by UNESCO to discuss the problem. The essential paragraphs are the following:

There is great genetic diversity among human populations. Pure races, in the sense of genetically homogeneous populations, do not exist within the human species.

The differences between individuals within a race or within a population are commonly greater than the average differences between races or populations.

Certain physical characteristics possess a universal biological value for the survival of the human species, independently of the environment where they live. The differences on which racial classification are based do not affect those characteristics; therefore, it is not possible to speak, from a biological viewpoint, of racial superiority or inferiority.

As a whole, it has never been proven that hybridization presents biological disadvantages. Quite on the contrary, it preserves the biological ties between human groups and consequently the harmony of the species in the midst of its diversity. The biological results of a marriage depend exclusively on the genetic constitution of the individuals forming the couple, and not on the race they stem from. Thus, there is no biological justification to forbid marriages between persons belonging to different races, nor to dissuade them because of racial reasons.

The world's peoples have identical biological possibilities to attain any level of civilization. The inequality of the achievements of the different peoples are due exclusively to their cultural history.

Certain psychological traits are sometimes ascribed to specific peoples. These affirmations may or may not be valid; however, there is no basis for attributing these traits to hereditary factors, until the contrary is proven.

There is no justification for forming a concept of inferior or superior races when we speak of hereditary capacities as regards intelligence, nor the aptitude for cultural development nor physical traits.[9]

DISCRIMINATION AGAINST WOMEN

An aspect of social discrimination which has not seriously concerned the biologist, since it has no rational biological basis, but which reflects certain phenomena of racial discrimination, is the relegation of women to a secondary or inferior level, something not unrelated to the problem of warfare. Both Simone de Beauvoir and Oliver Brachfeld have suggested that one of the main reasons for woman's inferior position, and the sense of inferiority that goes with it, is that she plays no traditional part in war.

It is well known that the warrior spirit tends toward masculine exclusiveness and contempt for women. As a result, certain warrior societies, such as that of Sparta, have favored homosexuality. In many Greek myths and legends the hero's rejection of a male companion for a female entails the loss of his warlike virtues, as in the story of Hercules and Omphale. Hitler had the same attitude: he prohibited women from attending the majority of German universities on the pretext that the atmosphere had to be "virilized" in view of the war. (Mussolini, more moderate, excluded women only from philosophy courses.)

Clearly, a world in which a lasting peace would be possible would be a world with a radically changed attitude toward women. Undoubtedly such a change in attitudes has already begun to make itself felt. Of course, there is nothing very new about the idea that women can be the salvation of the human species. Augustus Comte, the father of modern sociology, even planned a cult of woman, in order to free man from his violent masculine heritage.

But here, too, confusion of the social with the biological nourishes tenacious prejudices concerning the "inferiority" of female intelligence and of other female capacities. Women down the ages have suffered the same kind of social deprivation as Negroes and Indians; first their opportunities for self-realization, education, and autonomy have been taken away from them, and then the resulting deficiencies have been interpreted as innate.

The grounds for representing women as physically inferior are no better. If it is true that women in general are muscularly less vigorous than men (although there are some picturesque exceptions), women have more resistance to illness and to fatigue caused by ordinary conditions. It has been proven that infant mortality is always higher in the masculine sex than in the feminine. Furthermore, both physical and mental development proceed more quickly in women than in men.

In almost all general intelligence tests, girls are slightly superior until the age of fourteen; from then on the sexes are more or less equal, but females continue to display greater verbal facility. In the Allport-Vernon test of values girls obtain high scores in aesthetic, social and religious values with greater frequency than boys. Childhood stuttering is encountered between two and ten times more frequently in boys than girls. Women are more able to distinguish colors and are less susceptible to color-blindness than men.

We must conclude, then, that in the younger stages, when social discrimination has probably not had a chance to make its effect felt, females seem to be in no way inferior to males.[10] Men would be well advised to admit the inconsistency of their ideas concerning the superiority of their own sex, unless they are prepared to assume the risk that some day science may prove that they are actually the inferiors. Men, however, continue to point to the supposed inferiority of women's cultural achievements. The truth is that, in spite of the barriers women have always had to face, their contributions to civilization are too numerous to be questioned. It is probable that native crafts, source of the first technology and so, eventually, of science, were first developed by women. It is widely known that the first division of labor was along the lines of sex; in this separation women were probably left in more direct contact with fire and its applications, as well as with such basic techniques as weaving and the making of pottery. The importance of cooking has been completely ignored. However, it implies a tremendous saving compared to the time and energy that all other mammals devote to feeding, and it is logical to assume that this gain in leisure was an essential first step in the process that has enabled the human species to develop its techniques and knowledge.

If men are ever to recognize the true nature of women, they will have to change their own behavior in the process. Margaret Mead has called woman "the last slave of modern civilization." A world in which full scope was allowed to feminine values would be as different from the present one as a world that managed to do without war. There is no need, however, to assume that because it would be different any attempt to conceive what it would be like must be remote and utopian. We can draw inspiration from the Iroquois Indians who, although they have been deceived and despoiled on countless occasions, tenaciously continue to observe their solemn pledges, faithful to their ceremonial "oath-binding belts," and to the peaceful ways they have now adopted, and which they continue to follow, even though others do not. Another source of inspiration might be the peace rites of the Andaman islanders, with their evocative symbolism, their common mourning ceremonies, the role they assign to women, and their holidays of community dancing and hunting.

IS PEACE INEVITABLE?

It has been shown that the Pygmies who live in the heart of the jungles of Central Africa are the most peaceful inhabitants of the continent. Today, we may note, a number of Africanists agree that the Pygmies were the first inhabitants of Africa. Closer to us, the Scandinavian countries—in recent times the most pacific of all European nations—are also the countries which have developed, over this same period, a society in which poverty and despotism are least evident. If we are to have the audacity necessary to conceive a new and different order of things, it is important to recognize that the whole history of the human species is made up of examples of such audacity.

ETHNOCENTRISM

Margaret Mead tells us that in Samoa, when she applied the Binet test which consists of inviting the subject to trace the line he would follow to find a ball lost in a circular field, the young natives, instead of tracing the most direct itinerary, used the opportunity to sketch a beautiful drawing. Their aesthetic preoccupation was evidently stronger than their wish to solve the problem.[11] Various psychologists have also observed, after experience with similar tests, that it can be misleading to compare the speeds at which different individuals complete them, since there are groups for whom it is more important to work at a slow pace.

The cluster of traits one human group considers typical of another group, people, or race, generally without having any real knowledge of the matter, is called a *stereotype*. Fluctuations in public opinion are clearly reflected in stereotypes. In 1935, the majority of Americans considered the Japanese "progressive," "intelligent," and "industrious." Seven years later, these adjectives had been replaced by "conniving" and "treacherous." When Chinese labor was needed in California, the Chinese were judged to be "frugal," "austere," and "law-abiding"; later they were called "dirty," "repugnant," "incapable of assimilating," and "dangerous." It is easy to prove that such stereotypes are created by education and environment. A psychologist who had just come back to the United States from a trip to the Soviet Union showed a group of American children some photographs of a tree-lined street in Russia. In an unofficial report on the trip he wrote:

A boy put up his hand and asked "Why do they have trees along the streets?" A little confused, I turned to the group and asked: "Why do you suppose they have trees?" Another one answered: "So that people can't see what's on the other side." A girl had a different idea: "To give prisoners work." I immediately asked why some of our streets have trees lining both sides: "To avoid dust."

The most subtly recalcitrant prejudice is probably ethnocentrism. The most cultured and broad-minded person, capable of accepting both the biological equality of races and the relativity of his own cultural values, sometimes finds it difficult to accept certain habits or institutions found in other groups. Sometimes, prejudice of this kind even insinuates itself into the minds of social scientists. The most widespread ethnocentric prejudice is the European, or Western variety. To discuss it is always precarious. In the first place, all of modern science and technology is linked to Western culture. But all the non-western governments clearly want to share in the benefits of this Western scientific and technical knowledge. Thus Western ethnocentrism has gained a universal character without precedent in history. Accordingly, there is all the more need for the heirs of Western culture to realize that the Western way of seeing things is not the only possible one, nor necessarily always the best, and that there are more things in heaven and earth than are dreamed of in Europe's philosophy.

Unfortunately, it is difficult for any person influenced by this culture (which in our times means practically any cultured person) to avoid taking that small inadvertent step that consists in no longer judging Western culture as admirable because of its particular achievements, but rather in thinking that these achievements are admirable because they are Western. For instance, the idea of progress is a familiar one to Westerners, who therefore tend to believe that all progress is good. In the same manner many people who should know better believe that evolution tends to make man a superior being, and that even horses, given enough time, will end up by becoming men. Very similar is the belief that non-Western cultures are merely phases that the West has already gone through, and that are bound to evolve in the same direction as Western culture.

The ethnocentric version of cultural evolution has been answered by Lévi-Strauss with the same argument that biologists use to oppose the anthropocentric prejudice: mankind's cultural evolution, like the biological evolution of the species, does not proceed in only one direction. Mankind's evolution cannot be compared to someone going up a ladder. The only proper attitude to take toward the almost infinite diversity of cultures is one of gratitude and humility.[12] We tend, however, to look down upon the contributions of other cultures. For example, the Negro university of Timbuktú in the twelfth century could be favorably compared to its European counterparts of the same period. The same can be said of the general level of civilization in the three great Negro kingdoms of that age. Iron-working techniques, which are so important to Western technology, are probably a Negro invention.

Environmental factors make it very difficult to estimate the congenital capacities of human groups. For example, English authors often refer to Bengal Hindus as being "intellectual by nature," and to the Marathas as "inherently bellicose." The Bengal plains are chronically infested by malaria and intestinal parasites, while the Maratha mountains are relatively free of enervating diseases. It seems likely that both groups are being characterized by their respective climates. We must consider it fortunate for Western civilization that the

Romans did not decide in their day that our coarse barbarian ancestors, who inhabited areas that most Romans considered unlivable, were incapable of absorbing or creating a high civilization.

NOTES

1. E.K. Gough, "Changing Kinship Images in the Setting of Political and Economic Change Among the Nayars of Molabar," *Journal of the Royal Anthropological Institute,* 82, 1952.

2. As reported in Otto Klineberg, *Psicología Social* (Mexico City, 1965).

3. G. Turresson, "The Genotype Response of the Plant Species to the Habitat," *Hereditas,* 3, 211–350, 1922.

4. Y. Clausen and others, *Experimental Studies on the Nature of Species* (Washington, D.C., Carnegie Institute, 1940 and 1948).

5. As reported in Klineberg, op. cit.

6. M. F. Ashley Montagu, *The Concept of Race* (New York, 1964).

7. See Klineberg, op. cit., chapter 9.

8. E. Earl Baughman and W. Grant Dahlstrom, *Negro and White Children:* A Psychological Study in the Rural South (New York, 1968).

9. UNESCO, Document SHC/CS/122/8 *Réunion d'experts sur la race et le préjugé racial* (Paris, 1967). Re-

printed with permission of UNESCO.

10. See especially the numerous works on this subject by M.F. Ashley Montagu.

11. In UNESCO, *Le racisme devant la science* (Paris, 1960).

8

CAN WE DO WITHOUT WAR?

Our inquiry has led us to the point where it would seem clear that we must seek the true causes of war in something more recondite than man's conscious will or in the ends proclaimed by war itself. War may claim any end for itself, even peace. Motives and ends may change, but war is always the same. It is precisely this that makes many observers suspect its true causes lie buried below the conscious level.

One of the most serious modern attempts to understand war has been the study of the economic forces which influence it or its preparation. Modern nations have become increasingly conscious of the economic motives implicit in their conflicts; on occasions, they have even confessed them openly. Such was the case of the theory of living space *(Lebensraum)* so widely discussed at the beginning of the 1939 war. Nations today are very much aware of the sacred egoism of economic needs; to justify them, they draw upon biological considerations that are more or less Darwinian. The spirit of our age tends to admit socioeconomic arguments only to justify warfare, not to oppose it. But these arguments can finally be reduced to badly defined biological problems.

The biological case for war tends to run as follows. In order to insure the survival of any given group it is necessary to obtain—it does not really matter how—the means essential to such survival. Neighboring groups, which are usually other nations, are analogous to different animal species. Thus human warfare is a natural struggle for survival between different human species; there is no further need to justify expansion and aggression at the expense of those who do not belong to the same species as oneself. One is reminded that at the beginning of the Second World War an English political leader stated that when a British bullet entered the breast of a German soldier, this favored civilization and culture, the survival of which depended upon the biological survival of the British people. To this George Bernard Shaw had the courage to reply that when a British bullet killed a German soldier the same thing occurred as when a German bullet killed a British soldier: another death was added to the long list of war dead, a list as old as history.

The view of human warfare as just another manifestation of biological dynamism is persuasive because it appeals to an undoubted fact: many living species devour and are devoured by each other. But the glib phrase "the law of the jungle" does not describe even these facts adequately, let alone reveal the great variety of causes, some of them obscure, that can issue in human aggression. As a *justification* of war, theses of this kind are in the same class as the fallacious Darwinism that we have already criticized in other connections. When such theses are examined they invariably turn out to contain factual distortions, made to accommodate special pleading. One familiar argument, as Rapoport points out, is that wars are caused by economic factors. And yet it is clear from any rational economic calculation that a nuclear war, still considered a possibility, would benefit nobody.[1] Bouthoul points out that the city of Danzig, which the Nazis made such an issue of reclaiming, contained 200,000 inhabitants; the war in which they reclaimed it cost nearly 7,000,000 German dead.[2] One is reminded of the story that, after the fleet of Louis XIV had bombarded Algiers, the French naval commander was received by the Dey, or native governor, of the Turkish province of Algeria. "How much," asked the Dey, "has His Christian Majesty Louis XIV spent upon this expedition?" The Frenchman told him. "What a pity!" replied the Dey. "If the King had asked me to bombard Algiers I would have done it for one quarter of the amount."

Even if we accept the egoistical and pseudo-Darwinian position of considering no more than one's own immediate benefit, the terrifying waste that war brings in its train cannot be justified on grounds of economic advantage, no matter how sophisticated one's theory of the struggle for markets. This, of course, does not rule out economic forces as causal factors. Neither can they be eliminated simply because they do not justify war nor bring advantages to the winning side. The industries of war are roughly similar to those of peace, especially the primary metal and construction industries. In the great modern industrial countries, the general economic tendency is toward overproduction and the accumulation of capital. The production of armaments, Bouthoul argues, is the perfect solution to this problem, or has been so far.

If we accept this theory, war can be explained in class struggle terms as one of the ways in which the owners of the means of production exploit the productive process at the expense of the working class. Imperialism can then be seen as analogous to a class struggle between industrial zones and zones that produce basic resources. Thus the working classes of an imperialist country may share the warlike impulses of the capitalist class that exploits them.

The main shortcoming of this argument is that, even if it explains the wars of the industrial capitalist era, it is not in any way applicable to all types of war. For instance, how can the expeditions in search of Australian skulls or the "flower war" of the Aztecs be associated with the needs of economic production? We must not forget that Marx wanted to dedicate *Das Kapital* to Darwin, an honor which the latter declined. Although he was opposed to the Darwinist school of socialism, the idea of life in society as a struggle for survival was as obvious to him as to the majority of his contemporaries. Marx's theory of the class struggle had to have some features in common with the thought of the time. The difference was that for the Darwinian socialists, social struggle and war were eternal truths that had to be honorably accepted, though they could be made more humane. This stand was easier to take, even for pacifists, once they were convinced that they would become members of the race and of the class to which victory was guaranteed in these struggles and wars. Marx, on the other hand, did not accept the eternal necessity of social struggle. He saw the conflict between capital and labor as the last inevitable stage before the unification of mankind under one rationalized system. This would cause war and all destructive conflicts to disappear forever; only the tensions that promote dynamic, constructive competition would remain active.

Today, it is really not at all clear that the hope for peace lies in this direction. We know that too many irrational elements enter into the motivation of war, and that every time a rational cause or possible objective of war has been eliminated, war has found other reasons and other goals to justify its existence. This is why many thinkers have tried to investigate the irrational aspects of war more profoundly, and, rather than determining its ostensible causes and its overt ends, have tried to study its functions, especially its social function.

The brilliant French essayist and novelist Georges

Bataille, following the lead of his teacher, the anthropologist Marcel Mauss (who wrote a classic study of the gift and the social functions of wastefulness), pointed out the relationship between war and festivities.[3] This approach has much to recommend it, since it embodies many of the features that have characterized war in all ages and cultures: its sacred character, its irrationality, its collectivism, its glamor, its morals (quite unlike those of peace), its destructiveness. Festivities, Bataille points out, are characterized by a temporary suspension of the rules of conduct of the group and also by a temporary inversion of the sacred and the profane. This inversion he calls "transgression": in its extreme form it is a sacred orgy. Thus, in Rome, during the feast of Lupercal, slaves commanded their masters; during the *dies meretricum* ("Day of Whores"), prostitutes were honored by magistrates and priests. The more important the festival, the more we note the legitimate inversion of all law; it is indeed a sacred orgy.

The parallel with war is a striking one. Upon the outbreak of war, what we might describe as a reversal of values occurs. Brotherliness, human life, property, freedom, the right to disagree—all suffer a change in meaning. The category of what is sacred also changes in significance. Wars, like festivals, also imply participation in a kind of collective consciousness, which may reach the state of collective delirium—and there is nothing so unforgivable in wars, as at festivals, as failure to join in these totally irrational collective trances.

It is for this reason, as Tax has pointed out, that objective and rational discussion of the situation is extremely difficult in time of war.[4] If the war, whether just or unjust, is proceeding satisfactorily from a military point of view, critics of it are told that this is no time to show weakness of resolution. If things are going badly, on the other hand, they are told to stop being defeatist and to support their government instead. During periods of settled peace, with no conflicts in sight, there is of course no problem of peace. So the best time to raise the problem, if one wishes to be heard, is probably just before or just after a war, when the authorities have no excuse for accusations of cowardice or disloyalty.

A festival, Bataille makes clear, always involves gratuitous destruction of goods, and often of lives. Sacrifice at a festival is a spectacle, just as in war an exploit that in time of peace would be unthinkable exhibitionism becomes a hero's death. This sacrifice-spectacle quickly becomes more or less symbolic and aesthetic, with sacred images and national heroes being established as traditional symbols. In the early days of the cinema, the art historian Élie Faure predicted that films would come to play the same part in twentieth-century civilization as circuses among the Romans. It was no accident that the first truly successful screen spectaculars were Roman epics involving scenes of violence and torture. Contemporary television has profited from the movies' example, until war itself has become a form of entertainment.

Warfare, like festivity, somewhat resembles play. One of the many festive aspects of war is the unnecessary wastefulness of armed peace, or "cold war," a wastefulness that parallels the North American Indian custom known to ethnologists as *potlatch.* In the majority of cases, *potlatch* consists of the solemn giving of considerable riches to a rival by a chieftain, with the object of humiliating him, defying him, and putting him under an obligation. The recipient must cancel the humiliation and accept both the challenges and the obligation by offering another *potlatch* more generous than the first. In this way there develops a kind of arms race in generosity. But gift-giving is only one aspect of *potlatch.* In its more intense form, as described by Mauss, it includes a still more serious challenge: the solemn destruction of riches.[5]

When *potlatch* is carried out by a whole people, its purpose, as Bouthoul has emphasized, is to impress or terrify an enemy of that people: hence the parallel with today's arms race. Of course, there are other ways of getting an enemy to acknowledge one's superiority; the analogy between war and *potlatch* can be pushed too far. In order to expose all the functions of warfare, Bouthoul has proposed a systematic study of the destructive institutions of human society, and their relation to the general demographic situation. He classifies institutions of this type as follows:
(1) Institutions that prevent or impede procreation by segregating the sexes (prisons, forced labor camps,

monasteries, some educational institutions, armies, and others).

(2) Institutions that create unemployment, and so encourage emigration (under certain circumstances, war can be seen as a form of emigration).

(3) Institutions that debilitate, maim, and kill individuals (all penal institutions, including instruments of political and religious repression).

(4) Institutions that kill by mass destruction, such as the practice, common in antiquity, of population control through infanticide (war, if it has this function, can be called deferred infanticide).[6]

Bouthoul goes on to argue, on historical grounds, that when destructive institutions *other* than war have a strong grip on society, the destruction caused by war is only moderate. The liberalization of penal law has taken place during the very period when armies have been growing larger and war casualties increasing. *"Everything happens as if a balance existed between the group of modern destructive agencies on one hand and the demographic role of war on the other."* Nevertheless he does not posit a direct relationship between overpopulation and armed conflict. For instance, he feels that the Malthusian point of view oversimplifies matters, and points out that a strict Malthusian would have to consider poverty as the cause of war, when experience tells us that it is often associated with superabundance. An excess of population does not necessarily lead to war, but it does activate destructive institutions, of which war is only one.

Bouthoul considers that war fulfills a demographic and economic function that relieves pressure on the social structure and tends, above all, to stabilize the balance between population and resources. This would explain why we find war in thinly populated areas as well as in densely populated ones: an imbalance between the demographic and the economic structure can exist under either circumstance, and may have to be relieved by war unless other means are found. One of the most graphic examples he cites in support of this thesis is that of the monastic society of Tibet. Until the thirteenth century Tibet was controlled by secular rulers; then it suddenly became a theocracy, with all power concentrated in the hands of the monks. According to one estimate, the population of Tibet consisted of from 250,000 to 500,000 monks in a population of 3,000,000 to 4,000,000.[7] From this moment on, a new economic balance was established. The economic parasitism of the monks solved the country's economic and demographic problems so well that the standard of living of the Tibetan worker became superior to that of the Hindu or Chinese. The Tibetan solution was also adopted, at least in part, by the Mongols toward the end of the sixteenth century, when the invention of firearms and artillery caused them to abandon their plans for expansion. In general, it may be observed that an emphasis on monasticism checks population growth; monasteries and convents consume economic surpluses, which in other countries are destined for the maintenance of an army or for war preparations.

142

Can We Do Without War?

The leading characteristic of war in our times is that it has become total. The process began with the French Revolution, which introduced general conscription. Napoleon used to say that he could allow himself to spend thirty thousand men per month. Comparing Napoleon to Louis XIV, considered one of the most bellicose kings of monarchic Europe, Bouthoul points out that Napoleon had up to a million men under arms and Louis a mere 300,000, in a population roughly the same size. But this was a far smaller proportion of the population than the four million Frenchmen mobilized in 1914. And the impact of war on total populations has continued to increase. After the 1939–45 war, the government of the Soviet Republic of Byelorussia estimated that, of the ten million inhabitants it had in 1939, ten percent were known to be dead, and twenty percent missing. During the same war, Poland lost 14 percent of its total population. The losses, direct and indirect, of the war, including the war in China and the famine it caused, have been estimated at one hundred million dead. If we laid out all the corpses of those killed in war over the last three generations, they would stretch around the world 425 times.

The rise of modern technology has coincided with an enormous increase in world population. Perhaps life has become cheaper at the same time.

THE PERENNIAL QUEST

Where, then, may we expect to find peace? Is the search a hopeless one? There seems no good reason why it should be. Peace has coexisted with all the war delirium; it has even managed to survive its own innumerable failures. Nearly all peoples greet each other by some expression either of the wish for peace, or of the wish for health. This suggests that we unconsciously consider the loss of peace as a loss of social health. But while it is difficult to find apologists for illness—no one seems to have built any monuments to it or made it a prestige symbol—war has been exalted and adored throughout its long history. If it is true that the unconscious content of casual speech may express our obstinate hopes of peace, it is no less true that the parent word of "hostility" is the Latin *hostis,* which originally meant "foreigner," and quickly and imperceptibly came to mean "enemy."

The case of those peoples who, according to some ethnologists, do not know war, cannot, unfortunately, bring us much consolation. Throughout human history, in the overwhelming majority of cases, civilization has hardly appeared when war springs up to accompany it. As a remedy for human bellicosity, returning to the level of the paleolithic tribes is not a very promising suggestion.

We have to begin the quest for peace by facing the fact that our civilization has always been a warring one. Denouncing civilization in the name of peace is as pointless as denouncing history for the same reason. This has always been understood by the great religions, which have done much to promote the image of a lost and promised paradise where the peace that reigns is not of this world. At times they have gone so far as to support, at least in theory, a pacifist position in earthly affairs. It is true that on other occasions they have exercised merely a regulating and limiting influence—though this in itself is a great deal. Nevertheless, the religions that we usually consider the most spiritual, especially Buddhism and Catholicism, have been highly pacifist in spirit. If one or the other appears based on an older religious tradition which is less pacifist, as Christianity is based on Judaism, and Buddhism on the Hinduism of the *Vedas,* this demonstrates that there has been a progressive elevation and purification of the human aspiration toward peace. It cannot be denied, however, that Islam, another of the great religions, has been extraordinarily belligerent. Christianity itself, once institutionalized and converted into a religion of the State, not only intervened in conflicts, but constantly took sides, authorizing war in general when it supported certain wars. The papacy on occasion even instigated the hostilities. It is irrefutable, however, that during the Middle Ages the influence of the Catholic Church was very important in tempering, regulating, and containing the warlike advances of the feudal lords.

Religious leaders and confessional groups are not the only ones who have attempted to influence political activities in a peaceful direction. Since time immemorial, jurists have attempted to establish arbitration and systems of regulation that would either make violent conflict unnecessary, or stop it after it has begun. Most of the time, these attempts have done more to mitigate war than to suppress it. Since the Middle Ages numerous peace theories and peace projects have been elaborated. Their essential features are always more or less the same: an approximately proportional representation of the nations in a tribunal to whose arbitration they would freely subject themselves, but which lacks any power to impose sanctions that would prevent nations at any given moment from refusing to accept this arbitration. Such a scheme is based on the principles that war cannot be abolished, but that it can be reserved for use only as an ultimate solution.

All of this explains the successive failures of these legalistic plans. The most recent ones are well known: the Tribunal of the Hague, whose sessions were as listless as they were futile, until the declaration of war in 1914 made its devout lie superfluous; the League of Nations, which coexisted with Nazism, Fascism, and the Fascist suppression of a legitimate government in the Spanish Civil War, and found itself impotent in face of the Second World War. After this, the United Nations took certain measures which have had a limited degree of success in imposing its decisions on recalcitrant individual members. But the analogy between individual and collective conflict remains a poor one. Law is of little use when dealing with warfare, since it is impossible to control nations in the same way as individuals.

Many thinkers who despair of ever controlling or eliminating war by legalistic means have advocated instead a system of peace-keeping based on an international balance of power. Such a system is only a variation on the *pax Romana,* or imperial peace, which we have already discussed. True, it does not involve the actual occupation of foreign territory. But it does involve defining peace in terms of the capacity to make war. In other words, plans to achieve this balance are essentially checks upon one's own and one's adversary's aggressive appetites. In Europe, balance-of-power politics has been a constant source of minor conflicts that did not develop into major wars because victory for either side was seen to be too hazardous. But this outcome depended upon the existence of certain hegemonies or alliances, more or less invincible, that were capable of intervening at any time with sufficient authority to influence events decisively in their own favor. That is to say that this system is really no more than interventionism, and tends to become the deadening "imperial peace" of which we have spoken.

A type of peace theory related to the balance-of-power concept is based upon the theory of nationalities. The frequent occurrence of frontier and territorial wars has led some people to think that the solution might lie in establishing states based upon an authentic national unity of culture, language, traditions and race. Thus each nationality would remain happily at home and not meddle with the homes of its neighbors. The most one can say for this theory is that it is at best naïve, since the wholesale repatriation or self-determination of national minorities creates more problems than it solves, and at worst a disguised form of racism, with nationalities regarded almost as biological species.

An idea about the causes of war that hardly deserves the name of theory is that it originates in the internal structure of states. During the era of European monarchies, the responsibility for the initiation of war was attributed to this form of government. The general thesis was that the sovereigns sought war in order to satisfy their ambition, greed, or love of glory, or even in order to distract attention from internal difficulties and maintain their peoples in subjection. The defenders of this thesis forgot that the ancient republics had been extremely warlike and that, for long periods, the Venetian Republic and the Swiss Cantons had been the most warlike of nations.

Certain demographic problems, usually the overpopulation of the world or of certain regions, are frequently argued to constitute one of the causes which bring about warlike conflicts. If we examine population and life-expectancy charts for different periods we note a fairly constant increase in both (see Table 1), with an especially rapid rate of population growth in the twentieth century (see Table 2).

Measures to restrict demographic growth have been proposed and put into effect from the earliest times. In Japan before 1863, voluntary birth control, encouraged

TABLE 1

ESTIMATED WORLD POPULATION
AND DENSITIES, PERSONS PER SQUARE KILOMETER,

Years Past	Population	Density
1,000,000	125,000	0.00425
300,000	1,000,000	0.012
25,000	3,340,000	0.04
10,000	5,320,000	0.04
6,000	86,500,000	1.0
2,000	133,000,000	1.0
310	545,000,000	3.7
210	728,000,000	4.9
160	906,000,000	6.2
60	1,610,000,000	11.0
10	2,400,000,000	16.4

AVERAGE LIFE EXPECTATION (YEARS)

Neanderthal	29.4	Classical Rome	32
Upper Paleolithic	32.4	England 1276	48
Mesolithic	31.5	England 1376-1400	38
Neolithic Anatolia	38.2	U.S.A. 1900-1902	61.5
Classical Greece	35	U.S.A. 1950	70

Source: E. S. Deevey, Jr., 1960, "The Human Population," (Scientific American, 203:195-204).

149

TABLE 2

ESTIMATES OF POPULATION AND POPULATION INCREASE

Area	Population in Millions				
	1920	1940	1960	1980	2000
The World	1,862	2,296	2,998	4,330	6,129
Africa	143	191	273	449	768
North America	145	185	265	383	568
South America	60	89	145	256	422
Asia	1,044	1,278	1,706	2,532	3,560
Europe	461	541	593	687	778
Oceania	8.8	11.5	16.3	23.6	33.4

Source: *World Population Prospects as Assessed in 1963* (United Nations Publication, 1966), p. 32.

by the government, kept the population at about the same level. During this period, Japan did not undertake programs of expansion or aggression. This was no longer true after the policy of birth control was given up and the population began to expand. Bouthoul is so impressed by the Japanese example that he calls birth control "demographic disarmament."

But of all kinds of plans to achieve peace, those most commonly resorted to are probably disarmament plans. There are plans for total disarmament, limited disarmament, and for the simple prohibition of certain weapons (even the League of Nations took steps to forbid certain weapons and, surprisingly enough, some of its prohibitions were respected throughout the Second World War, particularly that of poisonous gases). All of these plans have their roots in the supposition that it is the possession of weapons that leads to war, and that the more deadly the weapons the more destructive the war is likely to be. Against this Bouthoul argues quite correctly that it is the manner and intent with which weapons are used that determine casualty levels. The greatest killings in history have been perpetrated by invaders possessing only swords, arrows and darts.

Barring the general use of bacterial and chemical weapons, there is no reason to believe that the development of more advanced weapons will necessarily lead to greater overall loss of life.

But what conclusions are we to draw from the fact that the plans for disarmament have never been fully applied? In 1888, following the advice of the Tribunal of the Hague, Uruguay reduced its active army by one fourth and Argentina and Chile each disposed of four warships. Even in such exceptional cases, disarmament is always only partial. Can it be that, even in the atomic age, mankind does not wish to end war? Will war be limited only sufficiently to allow humanity to survive and fight new wars, forever? This is the pessimistic conclusion of Bouthoul, on whose work we have drawn so heavily in this chapter. Whether or not we agree with Bouthoul, his historical and sociological perspective enable us to see how deeply rooted warlike prejudice is, and how impossible it seems that the chances for peace will ever improve.

But is there perhaps something here that has not been sufficiently emphasized? In the past, war has appealed to man's sense of brotherhood, even his sense of beauty. Today, technological advances have depersonalized war to such an extent that it can no longer be explained in terms of these traditional gratifications. If there is any hope, this may be where it lies.

NOTES

1. Anatol Rapoport, review of D. Carthy and J. Ebling (eds.), *The Natural History of Aggression,* in *Scientific American,* 213, 115-6, 1965.

2. Gaston Bouthoul, *Les guerres* (Paris, 1951).

3. Georges Bataille, "La civilisation et la guerre," *Critique,* 1951.

4. Sol Tax, "War and the Draft," *Natural History,* 1967.

5. Marcel Mauss, "Essai sur le don, forme et raison d'échange dans les societés archaiques," *Année Sociologique*, 1923-4.

6. Bouthoul, op. cit.

7. Charles Bell, *Portrait of the Dalai-Lama* (London, 1946).

9

A WORLD WITHOUT WAR

The facts generally adduced to support belief in the necessity or the usefulness of warfare, even when they are real enough, are always more or less ordered or interpreted to accord with our deep-rooted acceptance and even admiration of war. But science must necessarily attempt to be objective. As many arguments favoring peace as favoring war may be found, and to demonstrate the lack of rigor in the usual pacifist arguments does not necessarily imply that the opposing arguments are true. In the end, it is easier to seek facts that confirm our convictions than to change these convictions. As Bouthoul has shown, one may need less courage to face the dangers of war than to modify one's way of thinking; physical heroism is often accompanied by considerable mental and intellectual timidity.

IS PEACE INEVITABLE?

War is so intimately bound up with civilization as we know it that it is difficult to imagine a civilization based upon peace. Thus, with a tendency toward minimal mental effort, we prefer to search out the possible advantages of warfare, and provide ourselves with reasons that demonstrate the impossibility of a different civilization. Durkheim, one of the founders of modern sociology, finds that all human progress is the result of pacific factors within our society; however he also shows that war is universal, and cannot imagine it not existing. Other thinkers go further: they resist the idea that peace is the only source of progress, and refuse to believe that such a universal and characteristically human institution as war should be purely negative in its results.

Unfortunately, it is only too true that nations have never dedicated themselves to the cause of peace with the same single-mindedness that they have shown in the pursuit of war. The worldwide budget for war stood in 1967 at approximately one hundred and fifty billion dollars. In January 1968, the overall budget of the United States stood at one hundred and eighty-seven billion dollars, of which forty-three percent was for military expenditure.

It has been shown above how hasty interpretations of Darwinism have given an apparently scientific basis to this tendency. As late as 1942 Lord Elton said: "War, however much we hate it, is still the supreme agent of the evolutionary process. Blind, brutal and destructive, it constitutes the final arbiter, the text that the world has invented to measure the capacity of a nation to survive." Seven years later Sir Arthur Keith, one of the most noted anthropologists of the century, defended the evolutionary virtues of war, nationalism, race and class prejudice as agents of the biological progress of humanity.[1] In 1953, Darlington, the great geneticist, wrote: "Some men are born to command, others to obey, and others to remain at an intermediate level."[2]

We have seen that Ardrey, on the basis of studies undertaken by others, maintains a very similar position. For him also the struggle for existence in all its forms is both necessary and healthy "despite the sentiment," he says, "that has characterized education over recent decades and which has tried to deny the value of competition."[3] What is more, both Lorenz and Ardrey maintain that man possesses a lethal aggressive instinct. To reject these conclusions, as we must, by no means implies neglect of those studies of behavior which tend to clarify differential forms of behavior with a genetic basis. On the contrary, one type of research which most interests the physical anthropologist today is the study of "racial" or rather group differences, interpreted within a genetic and biological context rather than within the narrow limits associated with this or that nation or civilization.

On many occasions it has been affirmed that war brings certain benefits, notably the improvement of production techniques through the need to surpass the enemy's real or potential weapon strength, together with the contacts between isolated human groups that

155

would not otherwise have taken place. It is quite true that a number of great discoveries were made or perfected under the stress of war. One has to look no further than nuclear fission, which would probably have been achieved much later had it not been for the pressure on the United States to produce an atomic bomb before its enemies. Other more immediately useful discoveries such as DDT were also perfected with great rapidity in the course of the last World War. The argument, however, fails to convince. It is difficult to decide if progress of this nature is worth the cost of a war. It is also reasonable to assume that all these discoveries would have been made in time of peace. Indeed, they might have been made just as soon if so many men and so many resources had not been diverted to purposes that led only to their own destruction. Above all, it can be argued that while it may be true that war favors certain types of discovery, it almost always hinders the spread of the benefits derived from them to all mankind. Thus the Cold War has slowed down the advance of science, obliging research workers in different countries to study in isolation and to guard the secrets of their discovery in the fields of nuclear physics, cosmic navigation, and many other areas of scientific investigation. Even supposing that war did effectively contribute toward progress, any conceivable advantages it might have are utterly insignificant when set beside Bouthoul's demonstration that practically *all* those civilizations which have now disappeared were destroyed by war.[4] Of course, societies may crumble from internal causes, as Toynbee and others have pointed out. But it is usually war that finishes them off.

Nevertheless, this particular argument in favor of war has a perennial appeal. Indeed, warfare is now being referred to as *the* civilizing institution. Thus the sociologist Stanislaus Andreski writes that "human nature being what it is, without war civilization would still be divided into small bands wandering in the forests and jungles."[5] But what is "human nature," exactly? If it is something that necessarily leads to war, then why not argue that civilization has advanced in spite of war rather than because of it? Certainly, the benefits conferred by ruins and corpses are not immediately obvious.

Is war, then, a biological or a cultural phenomenon? Our view of war's inevitability depends on how we answer this question. Since 1940, Mead, Montagu, and other writers have maintained, without denying the possibility that biological factors are present in some degree, that war is a cultural product. In our opinion, the biological factors, should they exist, become daily less important; it is toward the rapidly evolving cultural phenomena that we must look in order to understand and solve the problem. The development of human weapons has overtaken those inhibitions against fratricide and genocide which are found in all other animals. Organized struggle between men has hardly anything in common with animal struggles: pushing a button to destroy an entire city is an act of a different type and on a different level from a blow with a claw, or even from the killing of one human being by another. If man has been able to overcome an instinct as powerful and universal as the respect of a species for its own kind, there is no reason to believe that he cannot overcome his supposed aggressive or destructive instincts.

We are surely lacking in imagination if we dare not give thought to a world without war. Yet there is no doubt that changes as profound as this have occurred in the evolution of mankind; human instincts as powerful as these have been transformed or replaced. The appearance of speech and writing and the possibility of accumulating experience are without doubt much more profound changes than the disappearance or transformation of any aggressive or destructive instincts. Another example is the birth of agriculture, by which man radically changed his relationship to Nature. If the tools invented by man in the course of millenniums enabled him to confront nature and benefit from her production, it was through agriculture that he discovered the mechanisms of production itself and how to control it. In other words, he not only benefited from nature—he changed it. This was a much more profound and radical revolution than the changes in our way of thinking which now terrify us.

The extent to which man can completely reverse an elemental instinct may easily be observed in the far more concrete and limited case of sex and reproduction. The organization of the family and its relationships, with all its complex rules, rituals and taboos, can hardly be attributed to biological instinct. No known form of primitive society is without taboos on these relationships. The most universal, the taboo against incest, was for a long period explained as a ritualization of instinctive tendencies, or at least empirical experiences, which would tend to unconsciously prohibit a practice so harmful to the species. Nevertheless, it is well known that animals have no such inhibitions—and this is entirely natural, since the study of genetics has shown that no biological harm can result from the occasional practice of incest. The only possible danger is that of the over-specialization that can occur in any small reproductive group if it greatly reduces its genetic stock. And yet no human society has a taboo against such a reduction; on the contrary, even today we have prejudices against the crossbreeding not only of different races but of social, religious, and ideological groups. The same genetic risks exist for a small white community, which does not intermarry with persons from other races, as existed within those ancient Egyptian royal families in which marriages were effected only between brother and sister. The taboo upon incest, then, is a peculiarly human creation, developed in opposition to biological or instinctive preference. It cannot be explained by studying animal behavior.

It is clear that the doctrine of evolution provides no excuses for our continued acceptance of warfare. We must have the courage necessary to conceive a different way of life: the courage shown by our most distant forebears when they abandoned the ecological niche in

159

which nature had set them and set off along the path of human development; the courage shown by the cave man when he learned to live with that terrifying agent, fire and, thanks to this, was able to change his food, his tools and his whole way of life; the courage of our remote ancestor who was willing to live in a world of language, symbol, myth and complex ritual, and dared to trust himself to that world and through it to the whole species, the common owner of this culture; the courage of the primitive agriculturalists who founded settlements and attempted to live in a new relation to nature, making laws and creating religion and civilization—and, finally, engaging in the organized activity that we call war.

In order to create this new thing, war, man evidently made use of all his biological conditions, instincts, and tendencies. That he should have done otherwise would be inconceivable. In all that man has done, he has utilized his biological heritage, transforming, altering, and rearranging existing components of it. It is for precisely this reason that man, spurred by desire or need, has always been able to find elements in that heritage that can be adapted to his objectives. It can be seen, then, that it is our objectives that are warlike, not the biological conditions that make us able to attain them. In order to achieve peace, harmony, and mutual cooperation, we lack neither instincts, arguments, nor conditions.

Our prejudice in favor of struggle, competition and survival has been carried so far that some even find a "struggle" in the relationships between the organs of a living being, the tissues of organs, and the cells of tissues. The relationship between a living organism and its environment has also been described as a struggle, and we are all familiar with phrases such as "the struggle against Nature," when it is evident that if mutual cooperation between man and Nature did not exist, man would surely perish, and perhaps Nature too. If we truly *struggled* against Nature, we would have perished long ago. Such a way of describing the facts is clearly anthropomorphic. But if it is an anthropomorphic interpretation that we want, it would be as reasonable to speak of "cooperation" between atoms and of "friendship" among cells. According to Charles Sherrington, the multicellular organism has evolved beyond the stage of perennial antagonism of cell against cell and constitutes a type of cooperation at the lowest biological level.[6] Other biologists have observed that gregarious tendencies are now found in unicellular organisms whose agglomerations are not based on any discernible goal, but rather on something that can only be described in such human terms as "sense of security" or "affective impulses."

Even genetic mechanisms can be described in these terms. In the mutation of genes, the changes that will become permanent are those that "cooperate" best with the total situation consisting of the organism and its environment. In any natural environment the mutual interdependence of all the organisms is a highly complex network in which every element is profoundly involved; the slightest local change will have repercussions throughout the entire system. The feeding cycles of the higher mammals, to cite one example, show how intimately linked is the entire plant and animal world. The "homeostatic thermostat" mentioned earlier (p. 90), is an inexorable law which prevents any deviation from a narrow limit of biological cooperation. Within our species, as within all species, the struggle for existence can never be a struggle against one's own kind. If individuals are restrained by natural selection, they can only be restrained in order to cooperate for the survival of the species. Our ancestors survive in us; we survive in our own descendants. This is true, of course, only in an impersonal sense. Since the direction that cross-breeding will take and the accidents of physical survival are both inherently unpredictable, biological survival is inconceivable at an individual level; it must be considered in terms of the different populations that make up the entire species.

As for the supposed natural superiority of some human groups to others, we have already seen that it lacks a genetic base, and that it cannot be linked to group survival. Nor can arguments from animal genetics be used in support of racism. The work of J.P. Scott is sufficient evidence of this. In fact, the rapid evolution of the hominids is undoubtedly due in great part to cooperation. Group hunting already implies a high degree of socialization, indispensable for the eventual appearance of the radical cultural change. In culture, strictly speaking, it can be said that cooperation (not exclusively biological, because we have reached another level, the cultural), is everything. Culture is a common heritage, a treasury formed by the contributions of all and belonging to none. It is the legacy not of nature, but of man, of one human generation to another. The originality of the human species consists not only in that it receives this legacy but in that it can itself voluntarily bequeath what it has voluntarily conquered and created. It would be difficult to find anything more essential and more characteristically cooperative than this voluntary giving of culture.

For this reason, in the human realm, all technology and behavior is necessarily cooperative. Thus every human being comes in contact with language, which cannot be acquired or developed alone; we inherit it not through the impersonal mechanism of the genes, but rather through personal instruction. The most visible human feature, intelligence, cannot be conceived of without this language, without this instruction, and without this common participation. The regulatory and ritual symbolisms of all human societies function to formalize the social mechanisms through which each individual cooperates with the other equally "initiated" adult members.[7] Hierarchy is not necessarily dominance or force; in certain activities it is also authority, and, equally important, it is a means not only for reducing aggression but also for promoting cooperation. There must be leaders for those activities that require an organized effort. Even in small societies, such as the Bosquiman and the Semang of Malaya, where there are no chiefs, one man assumes the leadership of certain activities and follows the elders' advice on camping. These societies, based on a hunting and gathering economy, do not have large cooperative groups; a man

163

hunts alone, or is accompanied by his son. The collection of beans or roots can also be done in small groups that do not require much organization. A more complex technology necessitates groups of greater cooperation.

This has been demonstrated by Firth,[8] among others. He found that, among the Maori of New Zealand, the simplest form of cooperation requires only two people working in the rocky channels of the coast. One holds the net close to the outlet of the channel and the other brings the fish toward it. The man with the net directs the operation. Nevertheless, to organize the conveyance of fish more men are needed. Usually a group is improvised to carry out this activity. The leader must be the oldest and most expert of the men. At times this fishing operation is performed by a permanent group, generally a family (here again we have evidence of the familial principle as a very marked characteristic of primitive societies). Even more people are needed to construct a large net in deeper waters. In all this, there must be a person to coordinate the setting of the net or the catch will be lost. This is a very simple combination of work; with the exception of the leader, everyone does the same thing. A more complex work combination would be required to set up a larger net. In 1886 a net nearly one-and-a-half miles long was used. It took several hundred men many months to make it. It had to be transported in parts and magic ceremonies were performed to assure its success. Two joined canoes with thirty rowers were employed to take it out to sea. The expert in charge of the operation mounted to the tip of a telegraph tower to give out the orders. Many thousands of fish were caught and the division of labor in this enterprise was much more complicated: there were net-makers, rowers, financiers. There were people on shore to hold the net down, the expert in the telegraph tower, and finally, the chief who initiated and stimulated the undertaking. Each activity had to be adjusted within the complex whole. Given the level of technology involved, it would be hard to find a more impressive example of cooperation.

The view of natural selection as a process that eliminates the weakest or the least apt is also excessively simplified. Natural selection does exist, but it is a phenomenon that must be very carefully interpreted and given its true value. Thoday cites the case of those who are color blind to red-green.[9] They are very much sought after by the dyeing industry because they can distinguish subtle shadings of color invisible to persons lacking this defect. He adds the example of a color-blind assistant in his genetics laboratory: this worker classified flies by number of hairs, not by color, and outperformed all the other assistants.

Our mania to discover antagonism in everything has gone so far as to conceive an antagonism between man and woman. The "sexual racism" (if we may forgive the term), which proclaims the superiority of the masculine sex, has relegated woman to an inferior position for centuries. Of course, nobody has reached the point of maintaining that woman is destined to be eliminated by natural selection. But such a proposal would not be much more absurd than some of the ideas about competition, aggression, and race which are considered worthy of serious defense.

A form of conflict that has received a great deal of attention in recent years is that resulting from the so-called generation gap. Some authors claim that no such gap exists; violence, they argue, is quite normal wherever there are rival ideas and ways of life, and any intergenerational differences are irrelevant as such. Others, notably Margaret Mead,[10] claim that the present younger generation is unique in being totally unable to accept guidance from the older because of the rapidity of social change during the past twenty years. I cannot bring myself to accept either view. On the one hand, I reject the notion of inevitable conflict. The crew members on board RA I and RA II were as different as possible in background, ideas, and temperament. However, they succeeded in getting along together. On the other hand, I do believe in the existence of a generation gap, not because wisdom and folly are nowadays distributed according to age (I think the distribution is much as it always was!), but for biological reasons.

Populations are made up of two or three generations, according to the usual definition of a generation as a twenty- or thirty-year age difference. As a population grows old and is replenished, it evolves. But it is the *population* that evolves, not any of the individuals composing it. Biologically, each individual remains the same throughout his life, dying with the same genes he had at birth. Genetic mutations do not show up until they are transmitted, that is, until the next generation. Most biological change, however, is due to the redistribution of genes through cross-breeding, not to actual mutation. But in either case, a type of discontinuity is introduced. At the same time, technological progress, especially the increasing scope and penetration of the mass media, insures that each generation to an increasing extent is exposed to the same cultural influences. Accordingly, there are two different *kinds* of processes that tend to produce a generation gap: the process of cultural standardization within generations, and the process of biological differentiation between generations. No wonder the generation gap widens every day!

Nevertheless, there is no need to conclude that every succeeding generation is going to be more hopelessly alienated from the one that preceded it. The history of evolution is neither more nor less than the history of how populations adapt. One generation's social and biological environment is not the same as another's, and it is unreasonable to expect any younger generation to behave as if they ever could be the same. It is a wholly remediable failure to confront the facts of socio-biological evolution that sets generation against generation, not evolution itself.

Man's aggressiveness has sometimes been attributed to his family relationship with the other primates, and sometimes to the biological differences which distinguish him from them. It is therefore necessary to recall that man's originality does not reside in his physical nature. It is not the lack of a tail which distinguishes him from the monkeys; actually, man has a longer "tail"— that is more coccygeal vertebrae, the remains of the tail —than the gorilla, the chimpanzee, the gibbon, or the orang-utan, which are the four large anthropoids. What really distinguishes man is the degree of social organization and cooperation in collective undertakings that he has achieved.

The following table of the differences between man and the other primates shows that the biological differences are only of degree; as animals, we are no more different from the anthropoids than they are from the other simians.

TABLE 3

	Monkey	Anthropoid	Man
Locomotion	quadrupedal	brachiating	bipedal
Thumb	small but used	small, used less	large, much used
Internal organs	adjusted to quadrupal posture	adjusted to upright posture	adjusted to upright posture
Sleeping position	seated	reclining	reclining
Rate of growth	slow	slower	slowest
Sexual maturity	2-4 years	8 years	14 years
Full growth in male	7 years	12 years	20 years
The male as food provider	never	never	main responsibility
Territory	small	small	large
Shelter	none	temporary nests	houses, fire, etc . . .

Source: Theodosius, Dobzhansky, *Mankind Evolving* (Yale University Press, 1962), based on data from Washburn and Avis' Chapter in *Behavior and Evolution*, edited by Roe and Simpson (Yale University Press, 1958).

Man is very like all the other primates as regards embryology, physiology, anatomy, composition of the

blood, and so on. Here are some of the specific characteristics that he shares with them:

> Large bones like those of the chimpanzee; stereo-
> scopic vision, with color perception; lack of mobility
> of the external ear; face rather than snout; reduced
> olfactory perception; loss of tactile hair; menstrua-
> tion cycle; no breeding season; birth of generally one
> offspring at a time; high degree of maternal care;
> domination of female and young by adult males.

The hand of the anthropoids is already specialized,
and shows similarities to ours. The hand of *Proconsul
Africanus* (of which we have the remains of several individuals belonging to the Miocene, that is, dating back
thirty million years) does not show the specialization
characteristic of anthropoids today, and may even belong to an ancestor of present-day man. The remains
of the hand found at Olduvai are about two million
years old; the hand seems capable of exerting a grasp-
ing force, but the precision of its possible activities
seems low.

On the other hand, the following characteristics distinguish man from the other primates:

1) Man has developed symbolism to a high degree.
2) Only man has a true language.
3) Only man is conscious of his own origin and biological nature.
4) Man is unique in his ability to store knowledge

beyond the capacity of the individual and beyond the limits of memory.

5) Man is the most adaptable of all organisms, having developed culture as a biological adaption. Culture evolves not in place of, nor differently from continuing biological evolution, but in addition to it.

As for man as a member of the animal kingdom, if he possesses any special characteristic at all it is precisely his lack of morphological specialization when compared with other animals. While some of our most primitive ancestors (*Ramapithecus* and the *Paranthropus*) possessed vegetarian teeth, the Australopithecines, who came later, have become omnivorous. We ourselves possess teeth suitable for a varied diet, without canines like the tiger's nor incisors like the shark's. We have neither the elephant's thick hide, nor the boar's fur coat. The bareness of our hands makes them inadequate weapons compared to a horse's hooves, a lion's claws, or a bird's wings. Our stomach is weak beside the goat's, which can digest almost any food. We have neither the keen nose of a hound nor the eyes of a lynx. Our great achievement is that, thanks to our cultural developments, we have been able to replace our biological lack of specialization with a cultural proficiency, while remaining biologically unspecialized and capable of adjustment to a wide range of environments. But our cultural specialization is peculiar in that, unlike the products of biological specialization, it can be changed, abandoned or even invented. Above all, human culture permits interchange and cooperation with others. The different specialized capabilities evolved by the different animal species cannot be combined, because the species cannot crossbreed. There is no such biological limitation on the "crossbreeding" of different human cultures, which together form a "genetic pool" subject to infinite combinations. All this is made possible by man's greatly developed capacity for using symbols. Human groups exist through the symbolic meanings that they share. Groups that are too exclusive, or that are sunk in mental inertia, will resent attempts to change their behavior or attitudes, and tend to become hostile to members of groups that they perceive as different from themselves.

One famous study provides a perfect illustration of this. A group of women factory workers was subjected to changed working conditions. The group's production dropped, but after about ten days it began to rise again. Then one member of the group reached the old production level. The other women were unpleasant to her, and their productivity slumped. Soon after, these women were transferred to another department. Their productivity immediately increased a hundred percent or more. Thus a small change in routine may be enough to overcome conscious resistance to innovation. The interpretation that psychologists give to this example is that the other women unconsciously transferred to the most productive woman their resentment of their changed working conditions. Surely we can overcome the prejudices that we direct against those who are so different from us that they fall victim to our mental inertia and our ingrained fear of change.

At the annual meeting of 1962-63 of the American Association for the Advancement of Science, among the thousands of papers presented, two were of special interest. One contained a review of all the biological species which have become extinct, the other dealt with now-extinct human tribes. Both papers sought to isolate the common characteristics which could account for this failure to survive. In each case the conclusion reached was that the extinct biological species and the extinct human species perished for one and the same reason: overspecialization.[11]

We have observed how the degradation of an opponent as something inhuman brings us nearer to a parallel between war and a concept that is valid in biological terms: predatory behavior toward different species, a principle that necessarily rules the whole animal kingdom, including *Homo sapiens,* and has as its most attractive manifestation agricultural exploitation of the vegetable kingdom. Treating the opponent as inhuman, that is, as a member of another species, was an important factor in the near-annihilation of the American Indian: saying that they lived like beasts, white Americans found it proper to treat them like beasts. Many other wars have been rationalized in the same terms.

Today, the diversity of human culture, the basis of

man's plasticity and lack of fixed specialization, seems to be threatened not only by the mutual incomprehension of different human groups, but even by a certain type of culture that tends toward uniformity and homogenization. This new culture is a product of the ever growing closeness of communities on our planet. It is difficult to grasp whether this process is beneficial or not. There is a paradox here which may be expressed as follows: in order to progress, men must collaborate; in the course of this collaboration, they observe the gradual homogenization of those contributions whose very initial diversity was precisely what made collaboration productive and necessary. To this Lévi-Strauss opposes the vision of a cultural diversity that is always reversing itself; a human species devoted to a single way of life is, he believes, inconceivable.[12]

The importance in human affairs of accepting other points of view can be observed on the individual level; for instance, Piaget has shown that the capacity of children to absorb group norms is directly related to their ability to deal with others on a give-and-take basis. Language itself obliges an individual to accept the point of view of other individuals and to adopt a standpoint which is not strictly personal.

A notable example of the reorienting power of language is reported by Margaret Mead. In an Australian reform school a teacher was trying to teach some aboriginal boys the elements of arts and crafts. Suddenly, one day a boy exclaimed: 'I understand! I understand! You do not draw things as they really are but as what they look like.' And the idea of perspective was born for the first time in his brain. The whole group then began to paint pictures with such originality that later a special exhibition of them was held in London, and the *London Times* devoted a whole article to the exhibit.

The most elevated forms of human thought and consciousness have been advancing towards a situation in which the concept of "other points of view" plays a leading role. Both reason and science are engaged in the task of eliminating pretensions to exclusiveness and conclusiveness. Western thought, rational and scientific as it is, today endeavors to understand and accept other forms of thinking; it recognizes that the first duty of intelligence is to be able to adopt another point of view, and that not even rationality itself is an excuse for exclusiveness. Thus modern ethnology has been making a tremendous effort to understand and even accept primitive, magical, and mythical forms of thought which are not based on logic or reason. Today, no ethnologist would even attempt to explain myths, rites, and archaic taboos as clumsy or naive versions of rational forms. The archaic myths are no less intelligent nor less coherent than our philosophy, with its worship of logic; they are a different way of thinking and of understanding the world, no less admirable and respectable than our own.

In the same way, the customs and social laws of other cultures must be understood without scorn or feelings of racial superiorty. All such structures, including our own, are relative; the only absolute cultural "inferiority" is the refusal to understand other cultures. For instance, the taboo against incest, so often cited as a cultural universal, takes on such different forms that we can find examples of different societies where the "sin" of incest consists in:

(1) Marrying a sister.
(2) Not marrying a sister.
(3) With a cousin.
(4) With the sister of an uncle.
(5) Not marrying the sister of an uncle.

What we are used to calling intelligence is also a relative concept; that is why no test can be devised to register innate intelligence, since no people can assume that their concept of intelligence is more universally valid than their neighbors.'

Man, who is simultaneously a biological and cultural being, is probably the most flexible form of life that there is. The cultural solutions which he produces are surprising in their variety, and it would be senseless to reject some as inferior; it is in this very diversity of cultures that the superiority of the human species consists. Men of similar races react differently in different physical and cultural environments. And yet very different groups sometimes produce very similar solutions to similar or even entirely different problems. The leading characteristic of culture is that its advances are many-sided. Man's capacity for devising symbols permits his imagination to conquer distances and apply systems designed for one purpose to other and entirely distinct purposes.

Bouthoul states that a biological function cannot be eliminated unless a valid subsitute has been found. "If we do not make war, what shall we do?" a chapter of one of his books is headed.[13] We believe that this writer endows war and the making of war with a biological meaning that, as we have seen, is far from relevant today, and which does not even reflect the history of war at all adequately. Warfare is not a biological necessity, either among the rest of the animal kingdom or among the species *Homo sapiens.*

Mead has recently proposed, in an essay that appears to me to be badly titled, something which does constitute a step forward.[14] She suggests that we put aside the tradition of obedience to outworn norms—military norms, for instance—and simply forget those aspects of the social structure which are no longer operative, such as the secondary role of women, the authority of elders in certain cases, and so on. Since past evolution, fully understood, is nothing other than the history of adaptation, we should strive consciously to adapt. The change civilization is undergoing in our days is for some thinkers as significant as the two or three most profound revolutions man has undergone in the course of his whole existence. The appearance of electronic computers, according to Leroi-Gourhan, is the final stage in the long process of what he calls man's "exteriorization." Thanks to the "exteriorized memory" provided by language and culture, man was able to slowly exteriorize all biological "techniques," from the knife-tooth and the hammer-fist to the laser beam that cuts and the nuclear blast that excavates. Today, says Leroi-Gourhan, it is the collective memory itself, the origin of the whole process, which is now being materialized in the electronic brain.[15] But neither the electronic brain nor any other technological advance will provide man with answers that he does not give himself.

We have seen that some of the most earnest inquirers who have concerned themselves with war consider that it fulfills a variety of indispensable functions in human society. According to them it would be necessary to find some way to fulfill these functions by other means. We have argued that, on the contrary, what man needs is a culture that has evolved to a level at which not even substitutes for war have any place. War is a social phenomenon, not a biological or a psychological one. Accordingly, to say that the problem of peace is intimately linked with the problem of social justice is not sentimental humanitarianism, but plain sociological fact. Man is possessed of a behavior specific to him, as the behavior of dogs or ducks is specific to them; he has concrete characteristics which have been transformed and which will continue to undergo transformation. One of these characteristics is that he is the only being who knows he is going to die. Given this knowledge, he can either abandon himself passively to the ebb and flow of natural processes, or work actively to control and transcend them.

What would a society without war be like? History offers enough precedents for us to make a few reasonable guesses. It would be a society characterized by a high and evenly distributed standard of living, one that had learned to balance production and consumption, and that could adjust its consuming population to its productive capacity whenever the reverse was not possible. In such a society, aggressive tendencies would be transformed through education into non-destructive types of competition. More important than the symbolization of aggression would be merrymaking, and all the possibilities for invention and culture implied by increased leisure.

Nothing that science can give us, that is, nothing that can be found in nature, can ever determine the future course of our history unless we decide that it should. What science does show us is that we must shed our prejudices and decide our own fate creatively, with imagination and courage. It is true that if we search our animal past we can isolate the conditions that have led to war. But war itself is man's invention, a product of civilization that we are justified in calling a cultural achievement, albeit a negative one. In that same past there are conditions that, if we bestir ourselves, may yet give rise to many other inventions. The creature that invented war can also invent peace.

NOTES

1. Arthur Keith, *A New Theory of Human Evolution* (New York, 1949).

2. C.D. Darlington, *The Facts of Life* (London, 1953).

3. Ardrey's views on competition and population control can be found in *Life,* February 20, 1970, pp. 48-61. To characterize these views as unscientific would be to pay them an undeserved compliment.

4. Gaston Bouthoul, *Sauver la guerre: lettre aux futurs survivants* (Paris, 1961).

5. *Time,* March 9, 1970, pp. 46-47.

6. Charles Sherrington, *Man on His Nature* (Cambridge, 1963).

7. Arnold Van Gennep, *Les rites de passage* (Paris, 1909).

8. Raymond W. Firth, *Economics of the New Zealand Maori* (Wellington, N.Z., 1942).

9. J.M. Thoday, "Geneticism and Environmentalism," in J.E. Meade and A.S. Parkes (eds.), *Biological Aspects of Social Problems* (London, 1964), pp. 92-106.

10. Margaret Mead, "The Generation Gap," *Science,* 164, p. 1222, 1967.

11. R. Buckminster Fuller, "The Prospect for Humanity," *Saturday Review,* August 29, 1964.

12. Claude Lévi-Strauss, "Race et histoire," in *Le racisme devant la science* (Paris, UNESCO, 1960), pp. 241-284.

13. Bouthoul, op. cit.

14. Margaret Mead, "Alternatives to War," *Natural History,* December 1, 1967.

15. André Leroi-Gourhan, *Milieu et techniques* (Paris, 1945) and *Le geste et la parole* (Paris, 1965).

FURTHER READING

Carpenter, C.R., *Naturalistic Behavior of Nonhuman Primates* (University of Pennsylvania, 1964).

Cohen, Yehudi A. (ed.), *Man in Adaption* (2 vols., Chicago, 1968).

Comfort, Alex, *The Nature of Human Nature* (New York, 1968).

Dimond, S. J., *The Social Behavior of Animals* (London, 1970).

DeVore, Irven (ed.), *Primate Behavior* (New York, 1965).

Fried, Morton, Marvin Harris, and Robert Murphy (eds.), *War: The Anthropology of Armed Conflict and Aggression* (New York, 1968).

Genovés, Santiago (ed.), "Statement on Race and Racial Prejudice," in *Yearbook of Physical Anthropology*, 15, 7-13, 1969.

Goodall, Jane, "My Life Among Wild Chimpanzees," *National Geographic*, 124, 272-308, 1963.

Howells, W.W., "Recent Physical Anthropology," *The Annals*, 389, 116-126, 1970.

Klopfer, Peter H., *Habitats and Territories* (New York, 1969).

Leiris, Michel, *Race and Culture* (New York and Paris, UNESCO, 1965).

Mead, Margaret, Theodosius Dobzhansky, Ethel Tobach, and Robert E. Light (eds.), *Science and the Concept of Race* (New York, 1968).

Montagu, M.F. Ashley (ed.), *Man and Aggression* (New York and London, 1968).

Shepard, Paul, and Daniel McKinley (eds.), *The Subversive Science: Essays Toward an Ecology of Man* (Boston, 1969).

UNESCO, *Four Statements on the Race Question* (Paris, 1969).

Washburn, S.L., and Phyllis C. Jay, *Perspectives on Human Evolution* (New York, 1968).

INDEX

INDEX

idealized in the Mundugumor tribe, 20

innate, 65

learned, 66

man's prehistoric remains as proof of his, 21

relationship of virility to, 4

remains of pelvis as proof of man's, 32

stimulus for, is external, 69

universal warring instinct seen as justifying, 19

war providing an outlet for, directed outward, 29

Alexander the Great, 29

Allee, W.C., 26

Alpon-Vernon tests, 124

Amazonian tribes, 22

American Association for the Advancement of Science, 172

American Indian, 172

Ammophila species of wasp, 79

Anatomy: comparison of man with all other primates, 168-169

Andaman islanders, rites of, 125

Andreski, Stanislaus, 157

Animal (s)

acquired nature of aggressiveness among, 53

aggressiveness between, related to territory and procreation, 44

aggressiveness dependent on level of social disorganization, 52-53

aggressiveness within the species, sex-linked, 44

combat between, generally a symbolic ritual, 45-46

competition between, during the mating season, 49

competition for the female, 45

complexity of the social life of the, 48-49

ferocity, prejudices regarding, 56

fundamental characteristic of struggle between, 53

males' aggressiveness, in defense of their territory, 44

mating season among, linked to territoriality, 55

order of dominance between, 49

"pecking order" established through conflicts between, 49

population density, 50

relationship between dominance and sex among, 49-50

restrained attitude of the, toward the defeated rival, 46

Animal behavior

investigation of, under natural conditions, 44

of higher animals in captivity, 43

science of, xi

Animal kingdom

mistaken deductions taken from the, 18

universal presence of war in the, 18

Antagonism, between man and woman, 165

Anthropoids

African, 52

and man, 167-169

characteristics distinguishing man from other primates, 169-170

complexity of social scales among, 49

dexterity of, 80

similarities with man, 169

the "Big Four", 55

Anthropology

current, 31

social, 70

Anxiety, war as relief from everyday, 28

Arapesh tribe

cooperation for common benefit in the, 20

gentle qualities idealized in the, 20

Ardley, Robert, 17, 69

Aristotle, 93

Armaments, production of, 136

Aryan supremacists, 120

Aryans, "socially superior", 97

184

Index

Index

Enlightenment, philosophical movement, 94
Environment
    group's adaptability to the, 41
    mutation to the genes help to adjust to, 41
    separation of heredity from, 83
Equality
    before the law, ix
    man's, defense of, 94
    of opportunity, ix
Erikson, E.H., 87
Eskimos, 19
Espasa-Calpa
    Universal History, published by, 36
Ethnic groups, war among, 89
Ethnocentrism, Western, 126-129
Ethnology, studies combining psychoanalysis with, 69, 174
Ethology, xi
Evolution
    biological, 82, 84
    culture subject to, 84
    Darwin's theory of, 33-34
    ethnocentric version of cultural, 129
    parallel between biological and cultural, 87
    "religion" of, 39
    sociobiological, 167
    two kinds of, 77-91
Ewer, R.F., 71
Exogamy, 102, 111
"Exteriorization", and electronic computers, 176
Extra-biological skills, for survival of animals, 79

Fascism, 146
Faure, Élie, 139
Feudal lords, warlike advances of the, 145
Firth, Raymond W., 164
Freud, Sigmund, 68
Frustration
    a stimulus of freeing of aggressive conduct, 67
    aggression depending on feelings of, 66
    Berkowitz and Holloway on, 67
    hypothesis of aggression, 73
    psychology of individual, 67-68

Galileo, Galilei, 34
Gelade monkeys, evidence of cooperation among, 57
Generation gap, 166
Genes, biological memory in the, 85
Genetic heredity, 83, 101
Genetic mutation, 166
"Genetic pool", diversity of traits contributed to the, 42, 171
Genetic selection
    and survival of the strongest, 41
    and survival of weaker individuals, 41
    in group crossbreeding, 40
Genetics, 72-73
    modern, 83
    science of, 102
    scientific meaning of struggle in, 41
Genghis Khan, 29
Genotype, 83
Gerontocracy, sacrifice as war motivation in, 26
Gibbons, 52
Gobineau de, J.A., 95
Goodal, Jane, 43, 79
Gorillas, 52
Goslings, experiments with, 54
Government by the fittest, principle, 99
Grant, M., 102
Greenlanders
    kidnapping of women, by 24
    unaware of war, 23-24
Group(s)
    adaptability, to the environment, 41
    congenital capacities of human, 129
    cultural, aggression between, 89
    ethnic, 87
    identity, during war, 27
    solidarity, during war, 28

187

INDEX

Index

189

INDEX

Moyer, K.E., 65
Mundugumor tribe
    maternal love in the, 20
    pride on being aggressive in the, 20
    sexual love in the, 20
    violence and aggressiveness idealized in the, 20
Mutations, triggered by Thalidomide drug, 84
Myrmeleon formicaleo, lion, 79

Nansen, F., 19
Natural selection
    eliminates competition within the species, 59
    idea of, based on Darwin's thesis, 96
    mechanics of, 51
    Noah's Ark, 51
    operating by automatic birth control, 89
    process of, 39
Natural superiority, idea of, 96
Nature
    balance of living forms and the inanimate in world, 41
    homeostatic equilibrium in, 89
    Huxley's concept on, 36
    John D. Rockefeller on law of, 37
    law of, 37
    maintaining a balance among living things, 41
Nazism, 96
    Gumplowicz seen as intellectual ancestor of, 38
    racist theories of, 96-97
Negro(es)
    —dolichocephalous men, 97
    kingdoms, civilization of, 129
    pamphlets on inferiority of, 94-95
Neolithic Age, absence of warfare in the, 20-21
New Guinea, 20
Novicov, Yakov, on social Darwinism, 38

Nuclear fission, 156
Nuclear physics, 156

Orang-utans, 52
Order of dominance
    and the balance in animal groups, 50
    between animals, 49
    evolved in mice, 53
    priorities for feeding and procreation, in the, 49
Overspecialization, consequences of, 172

Pacification
    loss of liberty as result of, 30
    of India by Britain, 30
    of Morocco, Tunis and Algeria, 30
    wars of, 30
Pacifism, 145
Papacy, the, 145
Papyrus vessel, crossing the Atlantic in a, xii
Paranthropus, 170
"*PAX?*" (film), xii
Pax Romana, 29, 31, 147
Peace
    as the only source of progress, debatable, 154
    at the price of slaughter, 29
    Aztec, 29
    conceived as:
        a natural condition, 17
        a positive state of things, 17
        an idealistic invention, 17
        something established through warfare, 17
        the absence of effort, 16
        "the first law of Nature", 17
    examination of the possibilities of a real, 16
    human aspiration toward, 145
    "imperial" 147
    —keeping on an international balance of power, 147

190

Index

linked with the problem of social justice, 177
perennial quest for, 144-151
theories and projects, 146
through war, thesis, 29-31
transitory, 16
"Pecking order", through conflict between animals, 49
Pharaoh Sesostris, 93
Phenotype, 83
Physiology: comparison of man with other primates, 168-169
Plants
differences in, due to environment, 113
genetic differences in, 113
Politics, balance of power, 147
Polyandry, 112
Population
and life expectancy charts, 148-149
densities in world, 149-150
enormous increase in world, 143
excess of, Malthusian point of view on, 141
losses in wars, 143
Potlatch, 140
Poverty and biology, 108-109
Power
balance of, 147
"pacifying", 30
Primates
characteristics distinguishing man from, 169-170
dexterity of, 80
evidence of cooperation among, 56
nonhuman, 81
Proconsul Africanus, 169
Procreation
—a factor in the aggressiveness between animals, 44
impeded by segregating the sexes, 140
Progress
impact of technological, on the military, 26

peace as the only source of, debatable, 154
war seen as a stage in human, 17
"Pseudospecies", 87-88
Psychoanalysis, 69
Psychoanalytic theory, on aggression, 68
Psychology, of individual frustration, 67-68
Pygmies, most peaceful people, 126

RA I and RA II, xii, 166
Race(s)
a changing biological phenomenon, 100
—a mystical and intuitive concept, 98
Aryan, 97
"colored", 114
concept of, 99-103
culture independent of, 105
ideas on unbridgeable hostility between, 38
Italian, 98
Lincoln on, 95
"master", 95
mixed, 95
prejudices centered on, 111-131
"pure", 95
"superior", 96
superiority of, 37-38
white, 95
yellow, 98
Racial prejudice, 95
Racial types, 105-107
Racism
called apostasy by Pius XII, 95
condemned by Pius XI, 95
fallacy of biological, 93-110
Hitler's, 96
so-called scientific, 95
—the most deeply rooted prejudice, 93
Racist theories, falsity of, 120-122
Ramapithecus, 170
Rapoport, Anatol, 88

191

INDEX

Rats
  aggressiveness of, 58
  experiments with, 52-53
Religion
  highly pacifist in spirit, 145
  of evolution, 39
Renaissance, romances of chivalry, 23
Renan, Ernest, 38
Repression, political and religious, 141
Reproduction
  order of balance discouraging, of animals, 50
  territoriality discouraging, of animals, 50
Rhesus monkeys, aggressiveness of, 58
Rockefeller, John D., 37
Rousseau, Jean Jacques, 94

Sacrifice, as war-motivation in gerontocracy, 26
Sadism, 70
Scalphunting, among North American Indians, 21
Schreider, Eugene, 102
Scott, J.P., 43, 63, 69, 162
Sea gull, 79-80
Selective process, Darwinian concept of, 36, 39
Self-justification, need for, 39
Self-preservation, instinct of, 47
Sepúlveda de, Ginés, 94
Sex(es)
"Sexual racism", 165
Shaw, George Bernard, 134
Sherrington, Charles, 161
Simians, 168
Sinanthropus, 21
Skin color, 103-104
Social deprivation, 123
Social groups, homeostatic theory of, 50
"social guillotine", 50
"Social uterus", 86
Socialism
  Darwinist school of, 136-137
  Marx's, 137

Society(ies)
  animal, aggressiveness in, 52
  anti-evolution, in Britain, 36
  crumbling from internal cause (Toynbee), 156-157
  feudal European, admission ceremonies in, 22
  genetically homogenous, —non existent, 100
  of Tibet, 142
  primate, 52
  warrior, 21
  study of animal, 52
Sociology, 123, 154, 157
Solidarity, group, during war, 28
Specialization
  cultural, 170
  morphological, 170
Spencer, Herbert, 37, 42
  Principles of Sociology, by, 38
St. Paul, 94
Stoddard, L., 102
Strength and survival, 33-42
"Struggle against Nature", meaning of, 161
"Struggle for existence", 40, 77
  Darwin's concept of, 36, 40
  pecking order—a direct application of the, 50
  role of environment in the, 40-41
Subjection, 148
Subjugation
  drive for, x
  of the masses, police in the, 37
Submission, finding fulfillment during the war in, 28
Subordination
  emotional, of men in the Tchambuli tribe, 20
  opposition to theories of, 34
Suchsland, Erich, 96
Suicide rates, during war-time, studies on, 29
Superego, in personality development, 81

Index

"Survival of the fittest", 40
    emphasis on competition and struggle in, 39
    genetic selection favors the, 47
    meaning of, 40
    neglect of cooperation and mutual aid in, 39
    process of adapting in, 40
    seen as the result of the victory of the strongest, 39-40
Symbols, man's capacity of devising, 175-176

Tax, Sol, 139
Taxonomy
    behavioral, 88
    cultural, 88
Tchambuli tribe
    man's subordination in the, 20
    woman's domineering role in the, 20
Territorial imperative, 75
Territoriality
    and the balance in animal groups, 50
    eradicated by domestication, in sheep dogs, 55
    instinct in man, 56
    mating season linked to, among animals, 55
    meaning of, 55
    strange forms of, among animals, 55
Territory
    animal males' aggressiveness, in defense of their, 44
    as factor in the aggressiveness of the animals, 44
    marking out of, by birds and fish, for survival, 44
    marking out of, by nearly all carnivores, 44
Testes, changes in, 64
Tests
    alfa and beta, 116, 117
    Alporn-Vernon, 124

general intelligence, 124
intelligence quotient, 118
language, 117
Thalidomide, drug, 84
Thoday, J.M., 165
Tinbergen, Nikolaus, 74-75
Toynbee, Arnold Joseph, 157
Tribunal of the Hague, 146
Turreson, G., 113

Unemployment, to encourage emigration, 141
Upheavals, domestic, hindered by successful wars, 24
U.S. Commission on the Causes and Prevention of Violence, 65

Vegetable kingdom, exploitation of the, 172
Vegetarian teeth, 170
Vertebrates, characteristics of struggle between, 53
Violence, eliminated by improving quality of life, 65
Virility, relation of aggressiveness to, 45
Voltaire, F.M.A., 94

Wagner, Richard, 95
War(s)
    a product of collective motivation, 25
    a world without, 153-181
    —a social phenomenon, 177
    acquiring benefits from, 24
    as events of strictly local impact, 22
    as part of man's culture, xi
    associated with self-sacrifice as well as with gain, 24
    biological necessity of, 89
    causes of, 133
    "cold", 140, 156
    conceived as:
        a natural phenomenon, 17
        a social disease, x

INDEX